TOP GOLF

Peak Performance
Through
Brain/Body Integration

Dr. Clyde W. Porter

Published by Life Enhancement Services

Published by Life Enhancement Services, Post Office Box 3236; Sparks, Nevada 89432

Illustrations by Tim Treanor

Library of congress Catalog Card Number 93-79602

ISBN 0-963 7669-4-5

TOP Golf℠, Performance Integration℠
T.O.P. Total Optimum Performance℠ are registered Service Marks

TOP GOLFERS Comment on their performance change following Integration.

I am finding that my swing is much more fluid. It takes a lot less effort. I don't feel the muscle strain I felt in the past. And being more fluid with my golf swing, the shots have become a lot more consistent in the fairway and accurate. I have probably increased my performance on the greens from about 12 greens a round to 14-15 greens a round.

Bob Hall, PGA Professional

I will say that I have increased the length in solidness of hits with every club in the bag. I'm probably a club longer throughout the bag of irons, consistently a club longer. I have been better balanced. I am swinging with proper mechanics now. I am not manipulating the club with the hand and arms to produce the shot I want; and consequently, it's much easier to manage a game because I know how far my clubs are going to go. After the Performance Integration^{SM}, without changing any of my work habits, as far as working on my game is concerned, my game jumped up a level.

Gaylord Rhodes, PGA Professional

Q. Have you ever done any other kind of program or practice or a mental thing that has affected you in the way this has?
A. No, I haven't. I tell you what, you read enough books in my profession and you see all these gimmicks come through back and forth, some of the subconscious things they talk about give you a tendency to understand your mental processes a little bit. But nothing that I have undertaken has given me the physical confidence that this has.

Paul Lane, PGA Professional

I found that I am making better contact with the driver, and the ball is going probably 10 to 15 yards longer.

Jan Usher, LPGA, PGA Professional

ACKNOWLEDGMENTS

I'm amazed at the human body. My first debt of gratitude is to The Designer. The second must be for the ability to extract from the body its machinations. What a remarkable study for myself and those other researchers who have been my mentors. To all of them, including Dr. George Goodheart and those who have expanded and taught his work, I owe deep appreciation for their sacrifice in discovery and their willingness to share. And my inspirer from the first, Dr. Bill Salsman.

Peter Wilday has not only been a stimulator, he has shared precious time and talent. Dr. Tom Kubistant has provided his own excellent research as well as advice. Capt. Ray Alcorn, U.S.N. Ret. and the aviators at Fallon Naval Air Station were willing and valuable participants in pioneer research in human performance enhancement. Nadine Phinney has for years encouraged and contributed support. What an honor and pleasure to work with the men and women who golfed their way into the research. Led by Allen Dunn these athletes came forward, open minded but skeptical, and put Performance Integration℠ to the test. Many are the respected acquaintances who read and critiqued the manuscript. And certainly, I'm grateful for the thousands of patients who I have been privileged to serve; you have taught me well. Yes, I have an office staff who greatly assisted me, Caralee Talbot and Melissa Hoadley. To my family who patiently awaited the final draft. And to all these named and unnamed, thank you.

PREFACE

A few years ago one of my patients asked me about her 9 month old son. The caretakers at this boy's nursery school expressed concern that her son was not physically mobile and crawling like the other children his age. He would only creep as a much younger infant. The child was otherwise totally healthy. My first thought, when an apparently "normal, healthy" human being acts contrary to an appropriate or expected level of performance, is that they are neurologically dis-organized. I recommended she bring him in for evaluation.

Indeed, the boy was tested and found to be "dis-organized". One harmless, light-touch, reflex integration treatment was given. The next day his excited mother reported that he had pulled himself to standing and was beginning to crawl. He quickly progressed after that. Magic!? Not really. Amazing, powerful, awesome, remarkable — yes, it is all of that! Incredible, unbelievable — perhaps to the uneducated. But this book will inform you about a new discovery which is changing lives.

Research shows that numerous individuals are burdened with a neurologic dysfunction called "dis-organization". The problem generally occurs with no clinical symptoms, and no apparent handicap, at least to the untrained eye. Yet, it influences virtually all functions of the brain/body, affecting everything from coordination to emotional stability. Now it can be corrected. I am excited for this discovery, this work, this opportunity for releasing the total person to achieve their full potential.

Every athlete who has been treated with Performance Integration℠ technology has had some kind of improvement in their athletic performance! That's some claim. One hundred percent is all of them. And emphatically yes, it *is* amazing, awesome, remarkable, but not incredible and not unbelievable.

Two years ago, I set out to research and gather data to support an excess of clinical anecdotes. Does the brain/body communication disorder we call "neurologic disorganization" cause performance problems? Do people who are neurologically dis-organized have some performance disadvantage? Do individuals who receive Performance Integration℠ treatment really perform better or "gain an edge"? More specifically — will golfers who receive the integration reflex treatment perform better? The answer to all these questions has been Yes!

Skeptical? Without exception all of the participants in the studies and testimonials in this book were skeptical. That's reasonable. If someone says to you, "you have a glitch in your brain/body communication that inhibits you achieving your full potential", you may feel your space is being invaded by some nut. But a simple muscle test can clearly demonstrate the problem. Further, stating that this previously unidentified malfunction can be harmlessly and quickly corrected may even seem more unbelievable, but all the evidence gathered here says, yes, it is correctable. Without a doubt, though, most remarkable and astonishing are the results of correction with a treatment call "Performance Integration℠." Astonishing, that is, if one, assumes that their body is "normal" and "as good as it can get."

I've seen integration treatment work consistently — innumerable times since 1985. Its easy to take your body and your performance for granted, yet, you really can be better. There is more to you than meets the eye — and if you are "neurologically dis-organized" you can have it corrected to release the Greater You. It is a matter of neutralizing that "glitch" in your computer program.

One TOP GOLFER is a 45 year old woman who has played golf for nearly her entire life. Shortly after Performance Integration℠ treatment, her playing and performance satisfaction were both markedly improved. She was truly renewed, invigorated and just generally excited about a whole new future in her golf game. She declared, though, with equal excitement, that after 45 years she knew where her feet were and she no longer tripped over everything in her path!

The little child who couldn't crawl and the 45 year old golfer who tripped over her feet had a common disorder — neurologic disorganization. And they had a common solution — Performance Integration^{SM}. Read about it, test it, try it. There is more to you than meets the eye.

FOREWORD

"Golf is played on a course of 5 1/2 inches — the distance between your ears."   Bobby Jones

There have been published literally hundreds of books on the physical components of golf. An increasing number of books are being written on the mental side of the game. Still, there has been relatively little research done on the most effective and efficient ways to integrate the body/physical and mind/mental to produce a consistent golf swing.

Well beyond our conscious thoughts and awareness, there is an intricate interplay between the mind and body. If one or both is slightly out of kilter, the golf swing will be ineffective and inconsistent. This explains why our swings may feel easy and rhythmical one round yet we feel like rank beginners the next round.

Many golfers feel that becoming aware and controlling this interplay between mind and body is far beyond them. Fortunately, there are answers. This book provides landmark information on how golfers can achieve that balance necessary to produce good golf swings.

Dr. Porter shares with us his research in Performance Integration℠ as it applies to the golf swing. It is extremely challenging to put forth principles and practices of brain/body reflex integration on paper. Dr. Porter accomplishes this task in fine form.

Read this book, but also feel what he presents. There are dozens of successful golfers who swear by what Dr. Porter has done for them. What he reveals in these pages works. I will leave it up to you, the reader, to find out for yourself.

Fifty years from now, I foresee golf historians viewing this book as natural and basic. Today for us, the information in these pages is groundbreaking.

This is a book to be read and reread. For serious students of the game, brain/body integration will be an essential addition to their game. The results achieved in your golf swings and scores will be well worth the investment of time and energy.

As you increasingly understand what Dr. Porter is presenting, you will learn what it truly means to "swing from center."

Tom Kubistant, Ed. D, CSP, Golf Psychologist

TABLE OF CONTENTS

Appendix

DEDICATION

To all who want
To be better
To do better
To have better
This book is for you

CHAPTER 1

GOLF AT YOUR PEAK CONSISTENTLY

Golf lessons teach the physical actions that increase the ability to make a good shot under various conditions. Good instruction and practice together increase the golfer's ability to make these good shots consistently. The golf instructor's efforts focus on demonstrating physical movements and conveying the mental instructions or language of the actions. Ultimately, through repetition, the brain/mental knows the instructions and the body/physical is trained in *what to do* to carry out the brain's sequence of commands to produce an ideal shot.

The "what to do" instructions or mental knowledge can be taught, and the physical "doing" can be trained.

What about the link between this mental instruction and physical actions? How efficiently and consistently are you able to translate your knowledge of "what to do" into the well-trained swing? Do you understand what to do, yet, the consistent swing still won't happen? Do you get some parts right while some element of the swing doesn't work even though you know what needs to be done? Do you sometimes get the feeling that you just can't seem to put it all together? Do you wonder how other golfers are able to "get it together"? Isn't there some way to improve this mental/physical linkage? Yes is the answer to this last question.

The classic analysis of golf is that it is a two sided game—physical and mental. All that we experience in the game, good or bad, is identified with one or both of these elements. Now, the technology of human performance reveals a third and all encompassing element. That element is *integration*. Integration is the oneness of the whole or the unity of expression. Integration concerns the communication dynamics of the brain/body and its synchronized, harmonious function. Integration is concerned with whether or not your body can respond to your message commands from your brain in a consistent, efficient way. Integration enables you to repeat your best performances and move to higher levels in your golf game.

A new and exciting technology of athletic performance has been developed called Performance Integration^{SM}. Amateur and professional golfers, after their experience with Performance Integration^{SM}, have noted the following:

> Increased power, greater accuracy, improved consistency, greater self-confidence, a better mental game, greater fluidity, lower handicaps, and much more.

Integrated golfers are consistently achieving higher levels of performance in their golf games and are experiencing greater self-satisfaction.

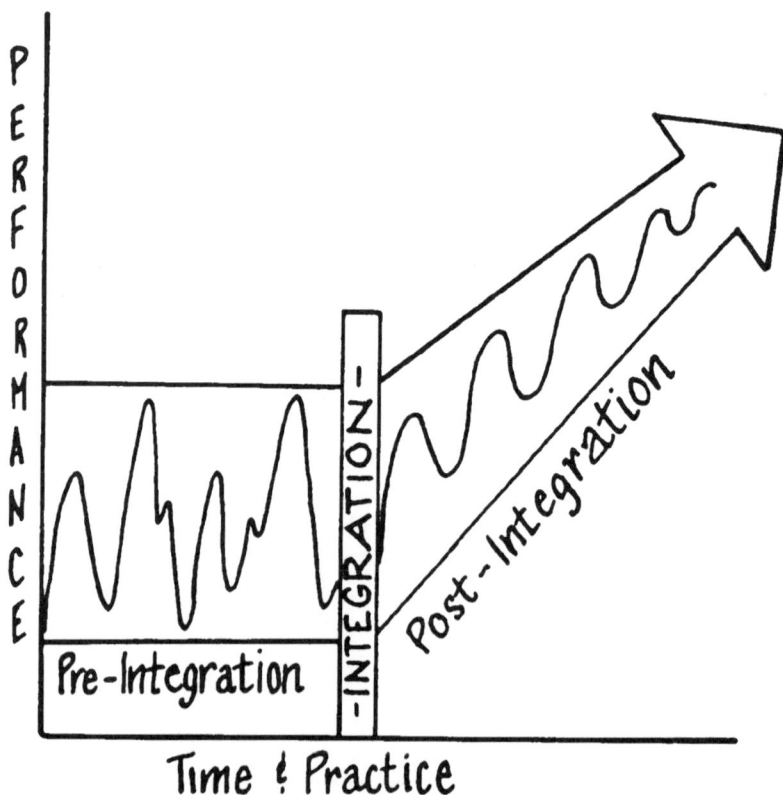

The real pinnacle experience in golf is being totally there, 100% in the game; brain and body on the same track. The play is consistent, dependable and ever improving. This experience incorporates the feeling of a focused and whole self. When one is integrated the mind and body operate as a single, focused entity, utilizing the whole brain. This state of brain/body flowing in synchrony is what allows peak performance.

FLOWING INTEGRATED GOLF

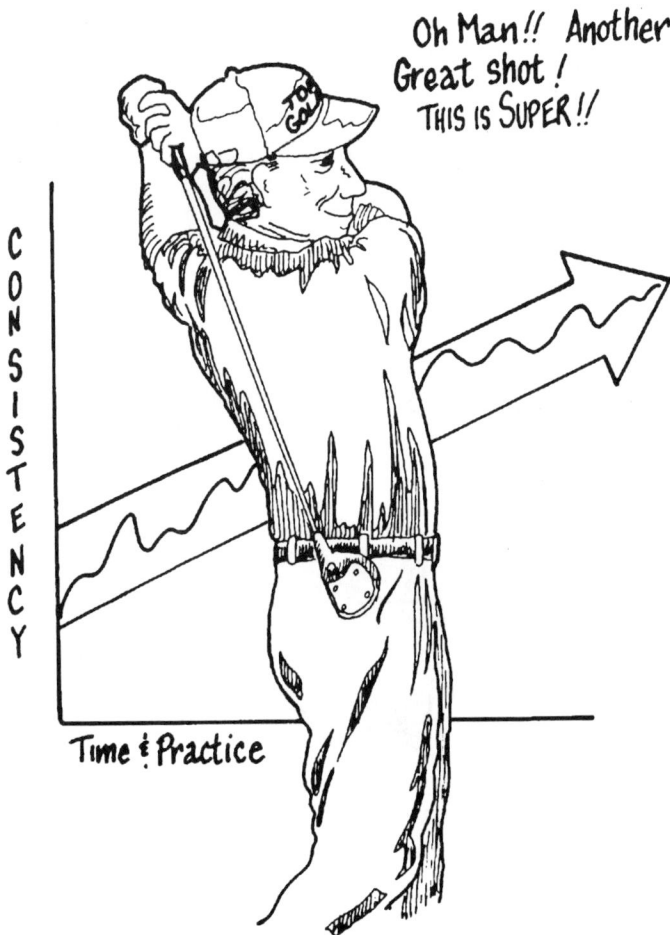

To be integrated is to achieve a state of wholeness. The channels of communication in the brain/body are open and flowing. There are no garbled messages, blocks or detours in mind to mind, mind to body, or body to mind communication.

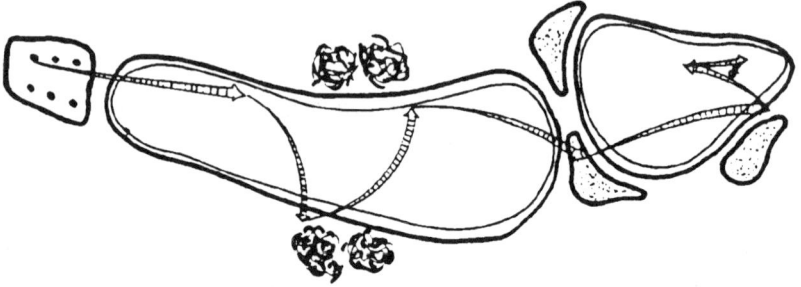

The disintegrated brain and body are out of harmony
Goal achievement is inconsistent and inefficient

Integrated golfers play with greater consistency and they achieve higher levels of proficiency in their game. Due to the harmonious cooperation of an integrated system, they get more rewards out of both their physical and mental practice.

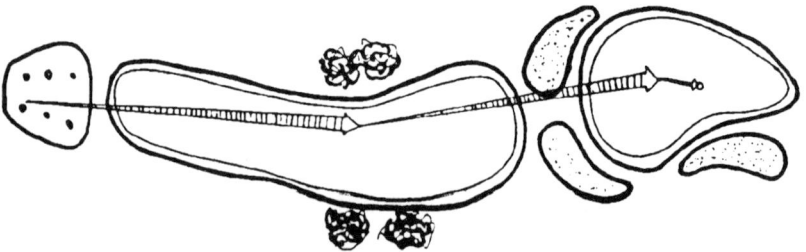

Integrated brain/body
Goal achievement without blocks or detours.

To master the game of golf one must apply physical and mental effort through their brain/body systems. All of the senses collect data and process it through the brain and apply it with the body. Just as we crawl before we walk, the brain/body puts together a program, step by step, to allow us to play golf. Progress and achievement are determined by all the data in the system and how well it is integrated.

PRACTICE   +/- ATTITUDE +/- INTEGRATION   = LEVEL OF
(PHYSICAL)   (MENTAL)   (BRAIN/BODY   MASTERY
                                COMMUNICATION)   OF GOLF

The natural tendency of the integrated mind/body is to improve at whatever task is being learned.

The brain is like a computer; it collects data from all the body senses and processes it for current and later use. Each of us programs our own brain/computer. Every person's body and brain are designed to function approximately the same way, but each person has personal variation and unique expressions. Notice that the swings of all the great golfers are slightly different from one another.

The brain has two sides or hemispheres. Some functions or processes are allocated to one side of the brain, while other functions require the participation of both hemispheres. It is critical in any pursuit to have access to and use of the "whole" brain.

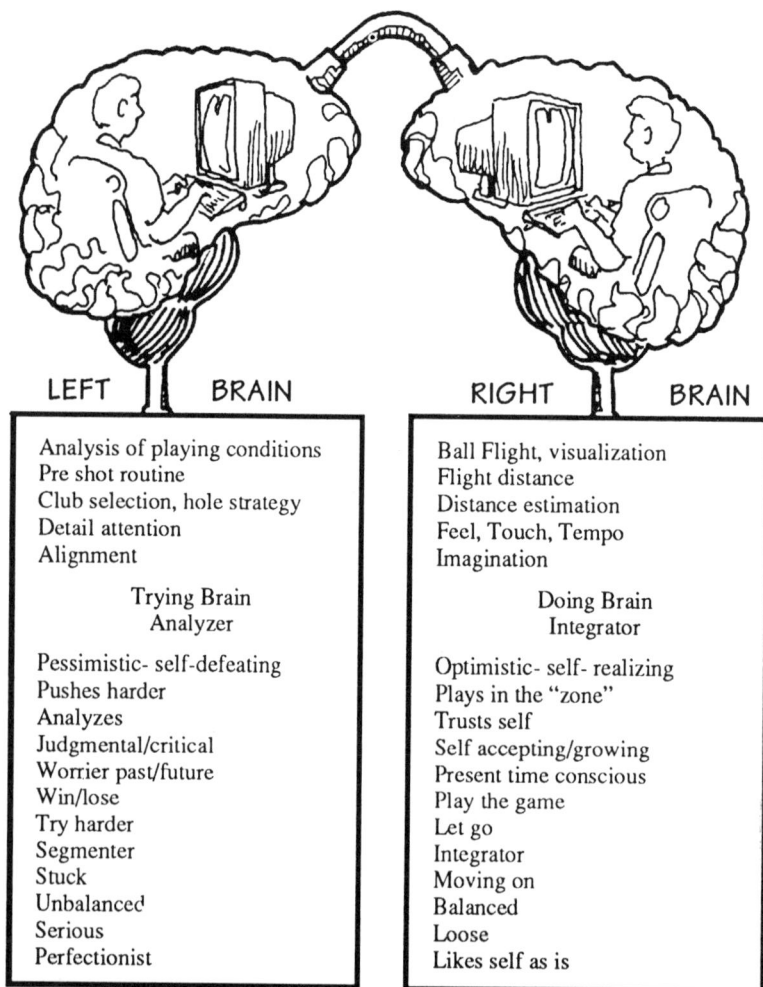

LEFT BRAIN	RIGHT BRAIN
Analysis of playing conditions	Ball Flight, visualization
Pre shot routine	Flight distance
Club selection, hole strategy	Distance estimation
Detail attention	Feel, Touch, Tempo
Alignment	Imagination
Trying Brain	Doing Brain
Analyzer	Integrator
Pessimistic- self-defeating	Optimistic- self- realizing
Pushes harder	Plays in the "zone"
Analyzes	Trusts self
Judgmental/critical	Self accepting/growing
Worrier past/future	Present time conscious
Win/lose	Play the game
Try harder	Let go
Segmenter	Integrator
Stuck	Moving on
Unbalanced	Balanced
Serious	Loose
Perfectionist	Likes self as is

Using a simple muscle test, one can determine if all parts of the brain and body are working together in a whole, coordinated, synchronized, <u>integrated</u> way. Muscles should respond on command in a crisp and consistent fashion. If they do not, it signals a communication breakdown or confusion in the brain/body system. This is called dis-organization or non-integration. In the non-integrated individual there are muscles which respond inconsistently to brain commands. Surveys show that most people have some level of non-integration. They are functioning with communication blocks, gaps and detours creating "No Go" signals in their brain/body system. This prevents them from achieving consistent high levels of performance.

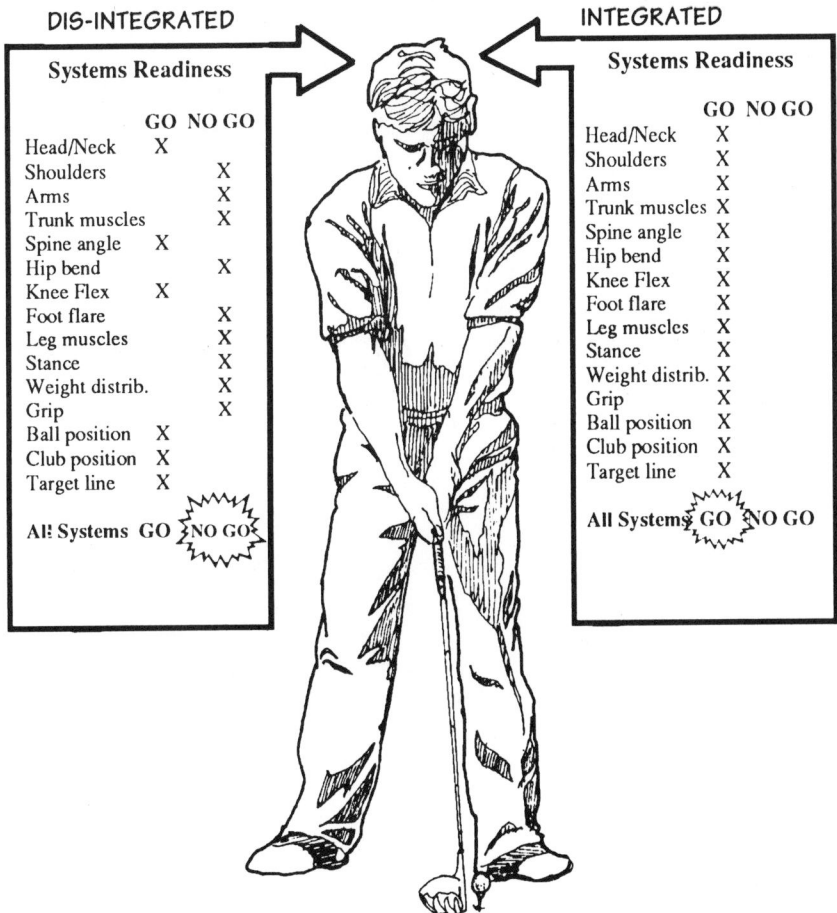

DIS-INTEGRATED

Systems Readiness

	GO	NO GO
Head/Neck	X	
Shoulders		X
Arms		X
Trunk muscles		X
Spine angle	X	
Hip bend		X
Knee Flex	X	
Foot flare		X
Leg muscles		X
Stance		X
Weight distrib.		X
Grip		X
Ball position	X	
Club position	X	
Target line	X	

All Systems GO NO GO

INTEGRATED

Systems Readiness

	GO	NO GO
Head/Neck	X	
Shoulders	X	
Arms	X	
Trunk muscles	X	
Spine angle	X	
Hip bend	X	
Knee Flex	X	
Foot flare	X	
Leg muscles	X	
Stance	X	
Weight distrib.	X	
Grip	X	
Ball position	X	
Club position	X	
Target line	X	

All Systems GO NO GO

The brain/body has two major states of activity. They are neutral or relaxed, and anxiety—fight/flight. Studies show that the anxiety reflex may be operative full time in the non-integrated individual. This causes various muscles of the body to be "turned on" or "turned off" at the wrong time. The body's very sophisticated computer allows mostly normal function in spite of this, but the subtle effects of this "stuck" program are still found. This reflex is not abnormal, but it is not normal for it to remain constantly in this state of non-integration. This causes brain/body performance to be inconsistent.

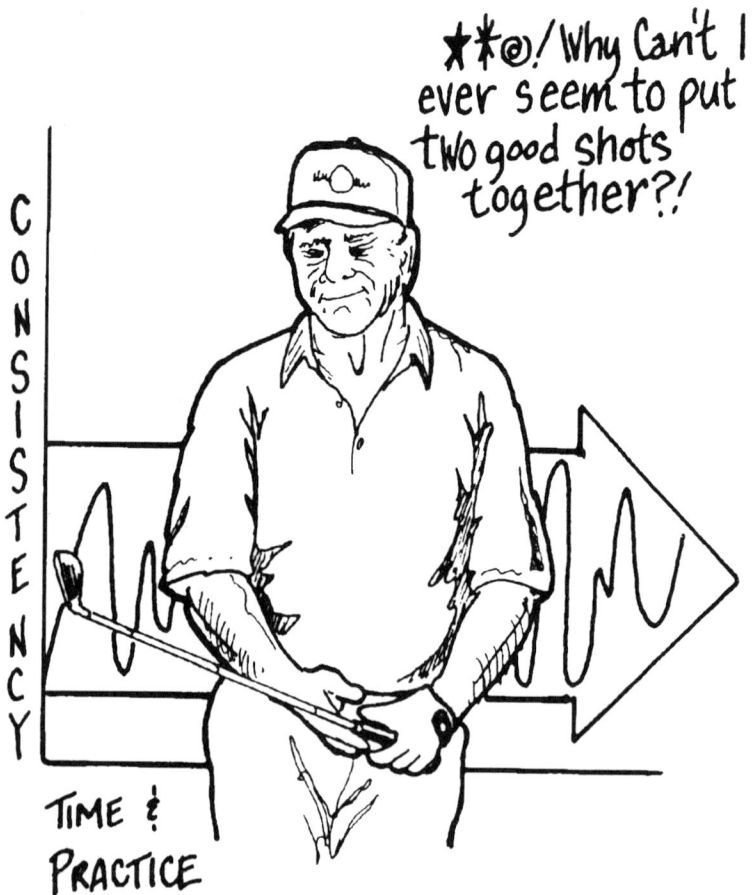

There is a typical pattern of muscles that respond sub-normally (weaker) in the non-integrated individual. Those muscles which test sub-normal are not responding in an integrated way. Most of the muscles of the body are used in the golf swing for power, balance, guidance, or all three. In the non-integrated golfer, these sub-normal muscles adversely impact timing, power, balance, coordination, consistency and more.

The non-integrated system also shows diminished communication between right and left brain hemispheres. This affects game management as well as other aspects of information processing.

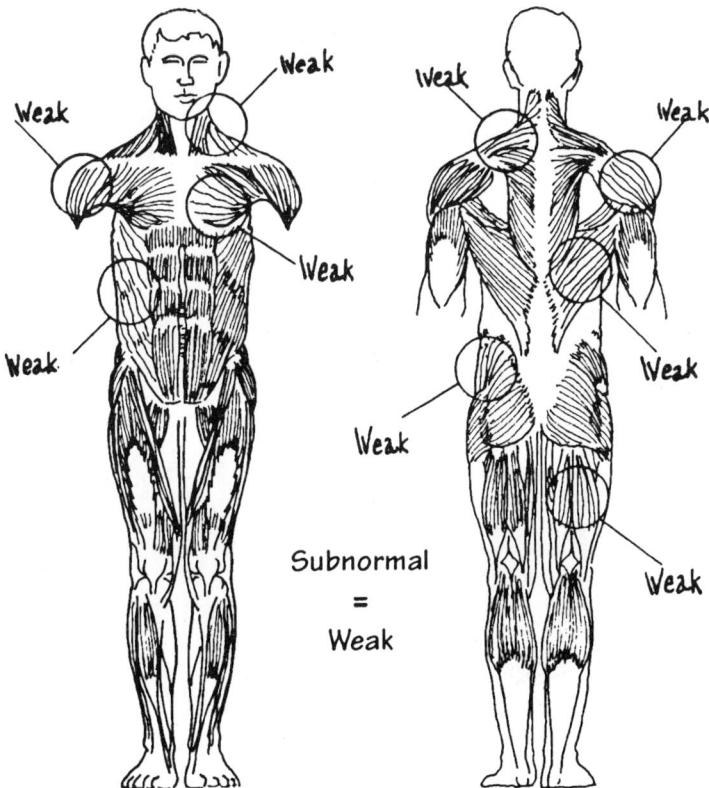

Muscle tests reveal confusion and inconsistencies in the brain/body communication.

The condition of non-integration is corrected with a body reflex technology called Performance Integration^{SM}. Over a three or four day period a series of brief treatment sessions release the stuck anxiety—fight/flight reflexes of the brain/body. This resets the brain/body to its neutral state. The results are permanent. Golfers who have been integrated report astounding results. This book thoroughly discusses the phenomena of neurologic dis-organization and its correlation with Performance Integration^{SM}. This short summary is primarily to introduce this revolutionary new discipline. Top golfers report the following experiences.

The Long Game

"I have a better feel for my driver. I am hitting the ball longer, and I am more consistently in the fairway."

J.M. male amateur

"I am hitting the ball longer off the tee. I used to be 20 yards behind some of my compatriots, now I am out with and beyond them." J.E. male amateur

"I am a lot longer off the tee." B.A. male amateur

"I gained 30 yards off the tee with increase of accuracy."

G.R. male professional

"I am more accurate with my fairway shots....being more accurate in hitting more fairways allows me to hit more greens in regulation. I have increased my performance from 12 greens a round to 14 or 15 greens a round."

B.H. male professional

The Short Game

"Instead of 35 and 40 foot birdie putts, I am more in the 8, 10, and 12 foot range." N.L. male amateur

"The short game has been a lot better. I noticed, markedly, putting had been changed, but more than putting, the chipping!" R.C. male amateur

"Chipping has improved as well, I seem now to be able to concentrate more on placing the ball rather than just getting it there!"
A.C. female amateur

Consistency

"The swing is much more consistent than before. I am more coordinated."
K.G. male amateur

"I find myself much more consistent now, much more pleased with my game."
N.L. male amateur

"I feel like I can go out and play and stay sharp from game to game without a lot of practice in between. And when you're as busy as I am that's a big bonus."
M.M. Male professional

Enjoyment of the Game

"I'm having the time of my life. I'm shooting better golf than I have ever played. (Handicap down from 14 to 8)"
J.M. male amateur

"It has surprised me that I am playing as well as I am because I haven't had a lot of time to practice or play."
B.A. male amateur

"After Performance Integration^{SM}, without changing anything as far as working on my game is concerned, my game jumped up a level. The balance is better, the performance is getting better, and its new. It brought some enjoyment back into the game."
G.R. male professional

The changes experienced by golfers receiving Performance Integration^{SM} treatment are remarkable. Without practicing or mental programming, performances improved in multiple areas of their golf games. This consistently occurs when golfers are treated for this common reflex problem called neurologic dis-organization. The correction is painless and permanent. The changes you have read about here are only a few of many experienced by amateurs and professionals alike.

It can be generally stated that Performance Integration℠ allows the brain/body to achieve wholeness or unity, allowing optimal performance. In this condition of oneness of brain/mental and body/physical, expect the golf club and game to be one, integrated with your intention and ability. Expect a level of enjoyment beyond any you've experienced in the game before.

POWER

ACCURACY

FLUIDITY

CONTROL

I knew I could make that shot!

Now I'll be on in two...

Play it high... don't overshoot....

...This is Fun!

	1	2	3	4	5	6	7	8	9			12	13	14	15	16	17	18	TOTAL SCORE
WEEK 1	5	5	5	6			7	6	5		6	4	5	7	5	4	5	5	90
WEEK 2	5	5	4	5			7	5	4		6	4	4	7	4	4	4	5	88
WEEK 3	5	5	4	5			7	4	4		5	4	7	4	4	4		5	87
WEEK 4	5	5	4	3	5	4	6	5	4		5	4	7	4	4	4		5	85
WEEK 5	4	5	4	4	4	5	5	4	4	6	5	5	4	7	4	4	4	5	83
WEEK 6	4	5	4	5	4	4	5	4	4	6	5	4	4	7	4	4	4	5	82
WEEK 7	4	5	4	6	4	4	5	4	4	6	5	4	4	6	4	4	4	5	81

CHAPTER 2

BEING TOTALLY THERE

INTEGRATION

Your body is essentially a machine operated by your brain/computer. The brain program, or software, is the guide or instructor which, through electrical stimulus, guides the motors and arms and levers and outputs of the body machine. The brain has 2 sides, or hemispheres. Each half operates the side of the body opposite itself. The right brain runs motor parts and senses of the left body while the left brain runs right body motion and senses.

In order to coordinate this very complicated body, the right and left brain must work together. They have to be synchronized, harmonized, and communicating clearly with each other. The right hand must know what the left is doing! The old adage, "He doesn't know his right from his left hand" can literally be true. If not coordinated side to side, the brain will not always communicate with the body parts clearly nor properly direct what the parts should be doing. "He bumps his head all the time"; "She trips on air"; or "He's a klutz" are common statements that reflect, unknowingly, that body performance may be imperfect, or that the body may not be expressing itself "normally". Even the most complex computer in existence, the brain, can have imperfections in output. When the two brain hemispheres lack synchrony, your body may not perform as it should. That word "uncoordinated" means "not working together". How can this extremely sophisticated and powerful computer not work together with the body? How can it allow the body to be uncoordinated, or to perform imperfectly in some way? This book deals with these questions with respect to learning the complex skill of golfing.

If you are not trained to do something or you have not learned it, it cannot magically appear as a talent, for example, properly swinging a golf club. Between never having played golf, and playing golf well, is a process of learning and coordination leading to some level of mastery. You sense how it's done with your own computer. With your body skills you duplicate what you are taught, told, or have sensed. Putting it all together, with a little training, you are able to become a golfer. Your brain/body then has a program for golf. A key point is that you program this skill yourself and you must continue to perfect the program to improve your golf proficiency.

What about the person who, for all appearances and through medical testing is found perfectly "normal", yet trips over their own feet, or confuses right and left? Or, perhaps, the person has trouble recalling what was learned yesterday, or can't read despite an abundance of teaching. These people might be great athletes but poor students, or vice versa. Perhaps they were slow to learn to walk, or a thousand other seemingly minor inconsistencies in the performance of the human machine. Is it attitude? Is it a training problem? Is this the way you expect a perfect computer to run the amazing body? Is the system designed to have inconsistencies?

Throughout history such things have just been accepted. "Johnny is a great mathematician, but he can't read well." "Mary is a super athlete, but she gets lost driving across town." It's as though this great computer truly does demonstrate inconsistency or "glitches" in its program. It skips a line, or leaves out a piece occasionally. Perhaps it can do math but not read, or it somehow may not properly communicate with the body. These inconsistencies in otherwise normal people are referred to as "neurologic dis-organization", or "neurologic dis-integration."

In order to facilitate a common understanding, we need to define some words and concepts. The verb "integrate" means "to make into a whole, unify, to make a thing entire". The related word "integrity" means "wholeness, entireness, unbroken state". In the context of our discussion, the word "integration" throughout this book refers to the whole brain, both sides, working together in harmony and synchrony with itself and the body.

What does "integration" have to do with golf, or the human condition? Interestingly, author Michael Murphy in his delightful book, *Golf in the Kingdom* (Arkana Pub.) touches on that relationship. He describes a small group of colorful characters sitting around a fireplace discussing the "true meaning" of golf. Here, Julian Laing speaks to Peter McNaughton:

> "Yer a livin' example o' what the game is all about. What is it but the comin' together of our separate parts? Ye said it yerself, Peter, just a little while ago when ye compared the game to marriage. Our inner parts want to marry too.

"I looked at Agatha (McNaughton). She was nodding in agreement, like many wives I have seen who pray for their husbands integration."(p.48)

Good golf is a product of physical effort or practice and requires coordination of the body through repetition of specific physical acts. It is also a mental game, affected by what we think or what action we originate in our mind. The "mental game" of golf includes the ability to focus, visualize, imagine, affirm, and the like. Integration is critical in those two parts of man, physical and mental, and in man's expression of himself in the game of golf. Another character in Murphy's story said golf was "the new yoga of the supermind" and said that with golf's technical modernization it "reflected man's ever increasing complexity" and was becoming a "better vehicle for training the higher capacities"(Ibid p.50). Well, why not? The refrain "golf is life and life is golf" follows similar reasoning. The story of neurologic integration tells us why this is so.

This book is about how we are physically integrated, how we are mentally integrated, and, finally, how these two aspects of the self and its expression in golf are integrated. This discussion considers the way your brain/body works as a whole, in a coordinated and synchronized harmony. It also looks at the integrity of your body's methods, purposes, and parts. Stated differently, this book discusses how your brain/body system works, how it may not be working correctly due to a natural error in your brain/body function, and how that error can be corrected, thus achieving integration. We are concerned whether you are functioning at your optimum best, or if a lack of integration is preventing you from achieving your peak performance. We will look at what may cause this and how this problem may be reversed.

This is a *new* discipline in human performance. We are dealing with how the brain and body work at levels that are, so far, unexplorable except for very young disciplines, among them Applied Kinesiology, which will be discussed later. We are reliant on the experiences of our fellow human beings who have ventured from the world of "neurologic dis-integration" into the world of "neurologic integration" and have come back to report. Most exciting are the results of a subtle but powerful new technique called "Performance Integration^{SM}". This natural, non-invasive, and non-toxic treatment virtually "makes whole" the normal reflexes of the human body. The treatment, which allows a restoration of the normal self, is a revolution in human performance engineering. The following experiences illustrate these concepts.

Jack is a 41 year old engineer. He is a working executive for a local corporation. His schedule is overfull including a 50-60 hour work week that requires frequent travel out of state, meetings in every sort of context, and paperwork/homework by the ream. He was a high school and college athlete and today still maintains a 15 to 20 hour per week workout schedule including golf, racquet games and gym workouts. He's also married, without children. (When would he have had time?)

His body and condition are that of a well toned athlete half his age, and his health is excellent. What's more, he's good looking and still has all his hair. This person is so close to perfect that other men his age are in awe of him. He is pleasant and well-regarded. In my own experience with thousands of other patients I must single this man out as one at the top of the ladder in ability and performance in most aspects of his life.

Using Applied Kinesiology muscle tests, though, Jack demonstrated neurologic dis-organization. That is, tests of his muscles that should have been strong showed weaknesses diagnostic of a brain/body communication disorder. It was a surprise to find these inconsistencies in what had to be classified as a man functioning at his peak. This finding of neurologic dis-organization or inconsistent brain/body response suggested that Jack was missing some personal edge and that there was more that his body could give him. He went through neurologic integration procedures and found that this was indeed the case. I'll not forget his eye opening report. Jack listed the following experiences a few months after his integration.

-No longer getting drowsy and falling asleep in business meetings
-Extensive work travel was not as debilitating on his body
-Homework in preparation for business was much easier and more
  productive

-Live business presentations were better organized and more
  effective
-Energy was higher and more consistent
-Lost a few pounds with no dietary change

This was an apparently "totally together" type of person who,
following a simple natural reflex treatment, was elevated to a new
and higher level of performance. Again, what impressed me was
seeing the best get even better and seeing a person near the top
gain a greater edge in performance.   Here was a natural treatment
designed to help heal the sick that demonstrated exciting results on
a top performer. To this I add my own experience. Six months
after receiving integration treatment I became markedly aware of
the following, not all at once, but, in an unfolding display.

-Right hand reflexes became quicker
-Left hand coordination with play and work was improved
-No longer able to maintain a slow burn anger
-Able to hit a baseball as never before
-Less easily upset
-Greatly enhanced ability to "think on my feet" in the way of
  organizing thoughts for private and public presentation
-Ability to perceive and experience feelings being conveyed by
  authors in my reading
-Exhilaration at such remarkable gains at the age of 40!!, without
  practicing something physical or mental.

So what does this have to do with you? Data has been collected on all types of cases before and after neurologic integration
procedures. The startling conclusion is that people who are neurologically dis-organized, no matter what their apparent level of performance, are not able to consistently perform at their peak.
Further, their current peak performance is below their body's
potential performance. And, the reflex protocol of Performance
Integration^{SM} can restore the body's ability to achieve peak performance more deliberately and consistently.

For eight years we have been observing the results of neurologic integration procedures on thousands of individuals. Early in

that time we noted the repeated occurrence of positive changes in people's ability to perform following integration treatment. Long term observations revealed improved performance and improved consistency in almost every case.

Recipients of Performance Integration[SM] report, with personal variations, the following common changes:

-Improved balance and coordination
-Improved ability to handle stress
-Improved ability to process information
-Greater self-confidence
-Greater self-esteem

Our most recent studies have focused on athletes and peak performers, particularly golfers. All treated golfers noted improvements in performance and/or well being. The overwhelming majority of golfers noted remarkable positive changes in their golfing performance. Most interesting is the vocabulary that they use to describe those changes. They report increased confidence, improved coordination, better balance, better game management (enhanced organization ability), and they are more relaxed (greater ability to handle stress).

This book is made up of the recorded experiences of those golfers; professionals, serious, and not so serious players. The methods and theories of neurologic dis-organization and integration procedures are also discussed. After reading it you will better understand the way your mind and body work. This alone can enhance your own performance. If you suspect that you are among those golfers who are neurologically dis-organized you will learn how to have that glitch in your computer reset.

The next chapter is a more in depth look at the phenomenon of neurologic dis-organization, its causes and effects.

CHAPTER 3

SYNCHRONIZING
THE BRAIN AND BODY

Proper neurologic integration of your body determines your physical coordination, ability to concentrate, ability to organize, self-esteem, self-control, self-confidence, learning ability, capacity for abstract thought, work allocation by the brain to the body, and everything else your body does. Functional neurologic dis-integration literally affects self-confidence by affecting the way the individual processes data and interprets it. The dis-integrated individual is affected in perception of their own body as well as how they relate to others. Physical self-control is broadly affected in subtle and not so subtle ways. This may be demonstrated as incongruities in coordination. Eye/hand coordination is compromised causing, for example, an inability to perfect motor skills. This can affect the golf swing or any other physical action. In spite of this dis-integration most people continue to function well. Remember, this computer and body are so highly complex that they have back-up systems for back-up systems. The whole purpose of this complex body is to survive and adapt—to "take a licking but keep on ticking". Many achieve high academic scholarship and even Olympic Gold Medals *in spite of* their dis-organization and resultant inconsistencies. Yes, they may function effectively at excellent performance levels but, if they are neurologically dis-organized, they will have *inconsistencies in performance somewhere. If improved performance is your concern, you will want to read further to discover why this problem occurs and how it is corrected.*

Neurologic non-integration affects many people. 70% of the population show some neurologic dis-organization when their muscles are tested by a trained specialist using Applied Kinesiology. Their brain and body are not in complete harmony and are not communicating as clearly as possible. This explains why a right hand literally may not know what the left is doing. The real time effect of neurologic dis-organization on the athlete is seen in their athletic performances which will be somehow inconsistent. That is, given the ability and training of a specific athlete, you expect a specific *level of performance.* You also expect a certain *consistency* in all phases of that person's athletic performance. To better understand how neurologic dis-organization might affect both the quality and consistency of the golf swing, read the following tongue in cheek description of the elements of the swing taken from Gallwey's "The Inner Game of Golf"

"ITS AN EASY GAME: Everyone can learn to play golf. Once a player has mastered the grip and stance, all he has to bear in mind, in the brief two-second interval it takes to swing, is to keep his left elbow pointed in toward the left hip and his right arm loose and closer to the body than on the left..and take the club head past his right knee.. and then break the wrists at just the right instant while the left arm is still traveling straight back from the ball and the right arm stays glued to the body...and the hips come around in a perfect circle; and meanwhile, the weight must be 60 percent on the left foot and 40 percent on the right foot at the start...and at just the right point in the turn the left heel bends in towards the right in a dragging motion until the left heel comes off the ground..but not too far..and be sure the hands are over the right foot, but not on the toe more than the heel...and be sure the hands at the top of the swing are high and the shaft points along a line parallel with the ground..and pause at the top of the swing and count one, then pull the left arm straight down, and don't un-cock the wrist too soon. Pull the left hip around in a circle..but don't let the shoulders turn with the hips. Now transfer the weight 60 percent to the left foot and 40 percent to the right...and tilt the left foot so the right side of it is straight..watch out for the left hand, it's supposed to be extended..but not too still or the shot won't go anywhere...and don't let it get loose or you'll smother the shot..and don't break too soon but keep your head down...then hit the ball. That's all there is to it!" (quoted in Gallwey p.46 source not noted)

It is a marvel how the body does all that. It takes the thought plus the body and *integrates* them to create the correct action. If the brain/computer and body are not in perfect harmony, there are many points in this complex activity where the golfer might experience some inconsistency in performance.

What if the golfer's brain is preoccupied or overloaded, mishandling information, short circuiting or simply leaving out a step or two? The problem of many well-trained, practiced, and capable golfers is inconsistency and hidden barriers to higher performance. In a majority of instances the player's problem may be non-integration or neurologic dis-organization. In other words, the golfer's reflex actions are not totally integrated.

Whether we are swinging a golf club, driving a car, riding a bike, writing a sentence or any other of life's very complex activities the non-integrated reflex system will show some inconsistency. The 70% of people tested who do show that their brain input to body output are not properly integrated have *inconsistent performance* somewhere, somehow, and sometimes. People with these performance inconsistencies don't individually demonstrate the same imperfections (or "glitches") in their body/mind performance. That is, different individuals don't show the same incongruencies when tested. This is because we all programmed our own computers. We all had different motivations, driving forces, sensitivities, perceptions, interests, teachers, methods of learning, luck and so on. Our personal computer input, processing, and output is just that—personal and individual, like snowflakes. That's called bio-individuality. This topic is discussed in the chapter on Performance Integration^{SM} theory. The inconsistencies are caused by a problem in the body called functional dis-integration, or non-integration. The functions of the body are not perfectly integrated. The word "functional" is used here because this problem is not about body parts or operations that are sick or well or missing, but about how they work.

Neurologic dis-organization is so subtle that it is often not observed. It has not been recognized as a problem. This suggests why little is known and less is done about it. We have come to accept inconsistent function as "normal". *The important thing to understand is this; given the power and sophistication of our brain/computer and the proper function of a human body, if they are communicating properly, there will be less inconsistency.*

Why aren't the effects of this condition more obvious? If most of us have these glitches and inconsistencies, why aren't we totally disabled? The computer/machine (brain/body) is sophisticated and survival oriented. It overrides, prioritizes, works around, fixes up, and creates a way to do what it has to do. Think of the power and ability of the world's great computers. Your brain-computer is greater. Add to this power the ability to think, reason, plus a motivation to adapt (win), it becomes awesome.

Yet what we have always accepted as "this is as good as it gets" is not the way it has to be. We are accustomed to how "adequate" and "normal" performance appear to us. We rarely analyze our performance and ask why there are inconsistencies. Through a natural testing method called Applied Kinesiology we are able to determine whether an individual is "integrated" in function. This study of muscle function reveals how a body is working. If a muscle shows improper function or weakness on the tested person's command, the brain is not communicating appropriately with the muscle. This weakness is a diagnostic indicator which leads the kinesiologist to a causative factor. When the cause of the weakness is corrected, the muscle will test strong as expected for a normal person. The performance of the muscle is then consistent with our expectation.

The origin of these inconsistencies of muscle function and therefore of neurologic dis-organization is believed to be a stressful incident. How your body handles stress helps us to understand the cause of neurologic dis-organization. The body responds to stress by action, internal and external. In a classic example, you are driving a curving mountain road in the dead of winter and your car starts to skid on black ice. Your muscles tense and brace, your arms and feet instinctively move to protect yourself from harm. Your teeth clench and your body may tense to receive an impact. Internally, your digestion and bowels shut down, your heart and your respiration speed up, and your glands secrete about a gallon of hormones to charge all these systems to handle the stress. Your body goes into the classic fight/flight stress reflex.

This is an over simplification, of course, but you've had some experience like this. Interestingly, this is a representation of your body reaction to stress no matter what the stress. It is the body's normal fight/flight reflex. Any threat to your survival will cause your body to assume some degree of this stress, anxiety, and fight/flight reflex. The stress could be a slip on the snow while walking, tripping up a stair, getting caught in an undertow at the beach, as a child having your father discover you scratched his car, or double bogeying your easiest hole. Your body has a programmed response to stress which is very complex, amazing, and predictable.

Now consider the stress reflex and neurologic dis-integration. In clinical practice using Applied Kinesiology, we discover that *people who are neurologically dis-organized demonstrate that their bodies are locked in this stress, anxiety, and fight/flight reflex.* The body/brain detours around the reflex to downplay and override it because of the overriding survival design of the body. Yet, the stress/anxiety reflex is running in the computer/body non-stop. The body is stuck in this fight/flight mode program as if running away from stress or danger. This posture includes stimulus (turn on) and inhibition (turn off) of appropriate muscles of the body to create running posture, tense clamping jaw, cranial and pelvic tension and locked gait.

This is the root of neurologic dis-organization. The brain/body is running a program which ties up significant software and hardware of the brain and body at the wrong time in the fight/flight reflex. This fight/flight posture is *not abnormal.* What is abnormal is that this reflex pattern is activated 24 hours a day causing the brain and body reflexes to be occupied, confused and "boggled", processing a normal stress reflex when it's not needed.

Remember that in spite of this brain/body dis-organization, function appears adequate because of the awesome power and complexity of brain and body which has back up systems, survival priorities, and abilities we haven't even thought of. Self-perception of what is "adequate function" varies from individual to individual, but generally only individuals seeking improved performance stop to evaluate themselves. Applied Kinesiology is a tool to assist that evaluation. Some people don't question whether their performance can be any better. This book is not for them.

How does disintegration happen? The best explanation is that trauma is the cause, such as a fall, a blow to the head, or bumping one's head as a child. Dis-integration can even occur in newborns due to birth stress. Minute movement of the cranial bones in harmony with other body movements is disrupted during trauma. These cranial bone movements must be synchronized with body rhythms to have the body function perfectly. A blow to the head commonly disrupts normal cranial motion, causing the body to go into the stress reflex. This is, again, a perfectly normal reflex reaction. What is abnormal is that the body remains "stuck" in the reflex. The sophisticated brain/body works around this chronic reflex allowing relatively "normal" function. This is how one effectively handles life in spite of dis-organization. Yet the effects are clear to the Applied Kinesiologist. Once integrated neurologically, a common realization is that the body is a much more remarkable mechanism than previously thought. The whole self released and performing normally is a wonderful instrument!

Perhaps you have this problem of neurologic dis-organization. Some functions of your body you may have questioned, but, without classical sickness or disability, you have accepted them as normal. No one ever suggested you might be non-integrated except possibly a parent who thought you were uncoordinated. You may recall inconsistencies in your performance while a child. Perhaps you are aware of an inconsistency that was noticed by others. The fact is your amazing body/brain has done very well allowing you to perform, function, and achieve in this life. Any inconsistency is only an occasional minor nuisance, overlooked, and now accepted.

Here's how the dis-organized brain may be working. If we ask the brain to travel from Chicago to San Francisco, it will obey the command if it is able. The route it chooses may be through Nashville, up to Milwaukee, west to Boise, back to Denver then on to San Francisco. It will probably accomplish the task, but in a roundabout, slow, and energy-sapping way. Why doesn't the brain choose a straight line from Chicago to San Francisco? What we believe is that the brain, like a computer, has certain types of routes to carry data, or wires, to pass information. In the functionally dis-integrated brain, the circuits and transmission wires may be occupied or overloaded. They are somehow unavailable for carrying information. The brain trip from Chicago to San Francisco may have taken the long way around with multiple detours in a poorly integrated fashion. The transmission lines are not broken, disrupted, or out of order. Rather, they appear to be occupied with other data transmission or program dedication. The brain is busy handling a stress response. The brain will most often get the assigned problem solved even under the worst circumstances (ie. get from Chicago to San Francisco). Occasionally the journey is not accomplished. Perhaps it's too slow and we give up or the data transmission appears to take a divergent pathway and gets lost and off track. This hypothetical explanation is based on thousands of clinical observations, and its purpose is simply to illustrate what possibly are the mechanics of the dis-integration demonstrated by the body.

What does this say about the normal function of the body? For instance, look at the task of swinging a golf club, batting a ball, or just walking smoothly. Neurologically dis-organized or not enough training usually can create some smooth efficiency in doing these tasks. Like the trip from Chicago to San Francisco the brain/body may perform a task with the most efficient, coordinated, and straight lines of communication or it may accomplish the task over multiple detours. It will find a way. *The dis-integrated nervous system takes the longer, less organized, more circuitous route, thus reducing efficiency, coordination, speed, and accuracy.*

Perhaps you have heard of people who are intelligent, study well for exams, and can't recall what they studied when tested. Or perhaps you know a well-trained athlete who can't perform consistently. Here's a clinical example. Doug is a junior in high school and a varsity basketball player. He loves the sport and is good at it. He's frustrated because of two things in his game; his feet get in his way as he runs down the court dribbling the ball, and, in spite of hours of practice, he can't consistently hit his 3 point shots.

Doug is physically normal, mentally able, well-trained, and well-practiced. He could be classified as above average in academics and this sport. So why do his feet get in his way as he charges down the court with the ball? Others do it well, why can't he? Isn't this inconsistent with the rest of his performance? Yes, it is. And why the trouble hitting the 3 point shots while others may do it well? Another inconsistency! The inconsistency is not a result of lack of mental ability, physical training, practice, or will. The inconsistency is a result of a brain/body output that is not in accord with predicted or anticipated performance.

What is interesting is that Doug, like so many other athletes, does not recognize the inconsistency or discordant performance as a problem. Why? It's not disabling and it's not unlike the performance of many others who demonstrate these inconsistencies. One of the *prime signs of neurologic dis-organization is performance inconsistency.* Doug, like most other athletes, was frustrated by this glitch or minor inconvenience. Yet he did not recognize it as a problem or malfunction until it was corrected. Following neurologic integration procedures the *inconsistencies disappeared effortlessly and without discomfort.* Doug now drives the ball across the court with greater ease and coordination. He also hits his 3 point shots consistently!

How significant are these changes? Consider the amount of effort, time, luck, practice, therapy, or whatever else you could do that would be necessary to change your balance, reflexes, or eye/hand coordination. Think seriously about how a person in their late 30's might experience a *real change* in their body reflexes. If a well-educated 40 year old man who has run 5-6 days a week for several years says "I have more contact with my legs", it is a *significant change.* If a very athletic 36 year old woman sees a "marked improvement in racquetball skills", it is a *significant change.* If within one week a middle-aged male golfer, playing seriously for years, has a "radically improved" short game after being integrated, that is *significant change.* Careful consideration of clinical results shows this remarkable fact, *people who receive neurologic integration treatment exhibit distinct, positive changes in their ability to perform athletically.* An observable improvement in performance reflects that the brain is apparently in better communication with the body. Something this subtle, yet so powerful, is difficult to quantify. A change in performance can mean gaining the winning free throw, returning the shot, cutting a stroke or two in golf, performing the athletic routine consistently or any number of other seemingly minor changes. *The high performance individual knows how important these "minor" changes are* and how difficult they are to achieve.

How else might someone obtain this type of subtle but powerful and significant change in performance? Look at these two primary methods for creating change in human performance.

Extended training: Changes in coordination or reflex time can sometimes be accomplished by days or months of practice and training. The more practiced athlete has an advantage over his equal match who is less practiced. He is able to reproduce a desired function more easily and consistently. Improved nervous system reaction due to repetition and body development increase performance ability.

Mental programming: Sometimes, with extended hours of cassette tapes, sports psychology, or mental imagery, one can improve performance. Mental training/programming is effective as it focuses intent and goal, supporting and sustaining the physical. We know that "what the mind can conceive and believe, it can achieve." Replacing negative thoughts with positive ones can also enhance performance.

Physical training and mental programming are rigorous. They require great effort, time, and discipline. They can provide some gain simply because they are generally a positive experience. Also, one's confidence is enhanced with any completion of a demanding goal or pursuit such as a training regime. Either or both of these activities are desirable and often necessary to upgrade or enhance any type of performance or function in life.

Yet, if the body can be freed from neurologic dis-organization it can enhance and surpass gains of training or mental programming. As a matter of important fact, *correcting neurologic dis-organization can cause all other training efforts to be more productive.* A common problem of dis-organization is the aggravating need to relearn and retrain a great deal at the beginning of a seasonal sport. The neurologically dis-integrated athlete is forced to retrace and retrain after the off season. A characteristic of the dis-integrated system, or the dysfunction of the neurology, is that actual relearning must take place at each new season. Because the mind/body functions do not *flow* naturally with the body in neurologic harmony, the athlete must *recreate* flow. Do not confuse "untrained" or "needing retraining" with "out-of-condition." Conditioning of the body and mind are essential to success in any endeavor, especially athletics. We have learned, though, that neurologically dis-integrated golfers have blocks and detours in their flow. This forces repeated re-creation of their ability along with conditioning of their mind and body. They must, at least partially, re-write the performance program every time they use it. When the blocks and detours are removed by Performance Integration[SM], the task of training is profoundly reduced and becomes a matter of reconditioning only, not retraining. The flow is not impeded in the neurologically integrated golfer. The lessons do not have to be "relearned".

Now, if an athlete is not integrated, but trains and conditions steadily, such as the golfer who plays frequently year-round, the blocks and detours of dis-integration are still there. What is not there is the forgetting of the body program by seasonal lay off. That athlete functions around the blocks, through the detours of disintegration and therefore has "flow" of sorts. They aren't repeatedly re-inventing their performance program. They may even be profoundly successful athletically. Still, that athlete is not able to flow/perform as smoothly or consistently as the integrated person whose brain/body is in greater harmony. It was interesting to learn from participating golfers that before integration treatment some game to game relearning had been necessary even when their golf games were merely days apart and not seasons apart. After neurologic integration they told us that they needed less warmup before a game. They found they were more able to get back into the groove after short or long lay offs.

> I have been a lot more competitive than I would have been playing once or twice a month in the past without practicing and going out and hitting a few balls every day. In the past it has been like I had to learn it over or go out and spend a couple days practicing. Right now, I can go out and play and stay sharp from game to game without a lot of practice in between. And when you're as busy as I am, that's a big bonus.
> M.M. Male professional

> I am very busy, so I haven't had a lot of time to play—- it has surprised me that I am playing as well as I am because I haven't had a lot of time to practice or play.
> B.A. Golf course manager

> I don't feel like I have to practice as much as I used to and still be able to go out and hit good shots and be confident all the time on the course. B.S. Male professional

> I feel practice comes easier, and I get a lot more out of my practicing. L.E. Female amateur

Performance Integration℠ is a truly remarkable neurologic integration procedure which restores your body's nervous system to neutral. This allows the brain/body machine to regain its full capacity to move you closer to a predictable, reproducible, 100% performance ability. The body's more natural and synchronized flow is restored. The brain more innately controls the body as opposed to "forcing" it.

Remember, your body naturally wants to give you 100%. It will if it can. The neurologically dis-organized brain/body balance is doing fairly well, but it is preoccupied with a fight/flight stress anxiety program that's operating 24 hours a day. This diverts the attention of the brain/body merely by its presence and occupies and uses body circuitry needed for top performance. Performance Integration℠ eliminates brain/body detours, opens up overloaded or preoccupied circuitry, sets new courses for data transmission, and restores efficient control of the body by the brain.

The power and simplicity of Applied Kinesiology and Performance Integration℠ is in the demonstration/experience of the pre–and post–muscle test. When tested, the person treated begins testing with apparent lack of total command over his muscle function. The person demonstrates "weak" muscle response indicating dysfunctional neurology. After treatment, muscles which tested weak respond normally, on command. They demonstrate normal functional response, telling us that the "glitch" in the computer program causing the body to function improperly is gone. The natural flow is restored.

This phenomenon has been demonstrated by Applied Kinesiology in clinical settings literally millions of times. For the *result-oriented* individual, the post treatment strong muscle response is remarkable evidence of change. That demonstration of properly functioning neurology carries the weight of numerous controlled experiments.

Performance Integration℠ has created measured changes demonstrated by hundreds of enthusiastic individuals. They have witnessed real and irrevocable changes in their own performance. These changes include increased speed and quickness, improved hand/eye coordination, better fine motor skills, greater strength, improved short and long golf games, greater stamina, less stress, and quicker response time. The list goes on. And the changes last. They are real and exciting yet they are nothing more than your body performing naturally as it was designed. A body that responds better to your command. A body restored to its more normal self control. A body that flows. The following are comments from post-integration golfers.

I have a better feel for my driver. I am hitting the ball longer, and I am more consistently in the fair way. I'm really in position where I want to be to hit the green.   J.M. male amateur

After the first couple of weeks, I started to strike the ball very cleanly, very well, and I am hitting the ball longer off the tee. I used to be 20 yards behind some of my compatriots. Now, I am out with them and beyond them.   J.E. male amateur

I noticed after the first treatment that my concentration increased. I was able to pinpoint more of what I was working on better which carried over into my golf game. I was able to concentrate on the ball and forget everything else. I am playing better now.   B.A. male amateur

Since (Performance Integration^{SM}) my balance has improved, and my focus has improved. I gained 30 yards off the tee with increase of accuracy, consistently at 260, 270, as opposed to a 260 then a 240. So it's a consistent distance now.   G.R. male professional

I am finding that my swing is much more fluid. It takes a lot less effort. I don't feel the muscle strain I felt in the past. And being more fluid with my golf swing, the shots have become a lot more consistent in the trajectory that I hit the ball and, of course, the accuracy.   B.H. male professional

I tell you what, you read enough books in my profession (golf) that you see all these gimmicks come through back and forth, but nothing I have ever undertaken has given me the physical confidence that this (Performance Integration^{SM}) has.
P.L. male professional

I went through the (Performance Integration^{SM}), I haven't had any lessons or anything since then, and I haven't seemed to be doing anything differently. I cut 5 or 6 strokes off my handicap in the process of doing it.   K.G. male amateur

Though little is known about the true inner workings of the brain, the testimonials of post-treatment athletes demonstrate that brain/body performance is changed by Performance Integration[SM].

A look at what we know about brain geography and work distribution can help us understand why neurologic dis-organization does what it does. Also, it shows us why certain changes are expected and witnessed when golfers experience neurologic integration.

CHAPTER 4

THE MECHANICS
OF YOUR
GOLF COMPUTER

In their book *The New Golf Mind* (1978), authors Wiren and Coop talk about the two-sided brain and its role in golf. They refer to the hemispheres as the Analyzer (Left Brain) and the Integrator (Right Brain). These terms are helpful to the understanding of the integrated golfer. Wiren and Coop separate brain functions in the following way.

THE TWO-SIDED BRAIN: GOLF FUNCTIONS

LEFT HEMISPHERE: THE ANALYZER	RIGHT HEMISPHERE: THE INTEGRATOR
Analysis of playing conditions	Visualization of ball flight
Pre-shot routine	Flight distance
Club selection, hole strategy	Estimation of distance on in-between shots
Attention to detail: lie of ball, grain of greens	"Feel," "Touch," "Tempo"
Alignment	Imagination on trouble shots

They further state: "For most mortals before good golf can happen, there has to be a solid partnership of the two brain hemispheres, one which permits analytical modes and intuitive modes of thinking to play equal and complimentary roles" (p.14).

A simplified look at this "hemispheric specialization" will help you see why performance integration of the brain/body is so critical to the optimum performance of the body. We are generally aware that the right and left hemisphere of the brain are somewhat different in the functions they perform for the body. That is, different body functions are handled by different sides or areas of the brain. This phenomenon is called lateralization. Functions of the body may be strongly lateralized being mostly controlled by one hemisphere of the brain, or they may be weakly lateralized such that both sides of the brain share some of a function. The notion that all brain activity is regulated hemispherically is useful to develop the model of neurologic order of the body, but this simplistic concept is only true in part. One side or area of the brain may developmentally specialize in various functions and give rise to lateralization. This leads to right or left brain distribution of duties and functions of the body. The complexity and nature of our body computer/command system is such that its feedback loops and backup systems allow hemispheric specialization. Lateralization is, in part, a matter of creating order and efficiency of function.

A great deal of the information on brain lateralization in humans has been derived from observation of subjects affected by head injuries or diseases of the brain such as tumors. Functions of the brain have been mapped by looking at the after affects of injury. For example, we observe that a stroke or broken blood vessel in the right brain cortex may cause paralysis of the left side of the body or vice versa. Motor control of body movement is, in part, bilateral with right and left brain hemispheres sharing responsibility, except for fine motor movements of the fingers. Research has shown that, for the most part, right brain controls the left side while left brain controls the right side of the body.

The majority of the body's sensory information (e.g., sight, sound and touch) is processed by the brain hemisphere opposite the body side on which the sensation is received. However, both sides of the brain appear to be active in some way in most information processing. Other methods of brain function analysis are providing further data on lateralization and hemispheric specialization which continues to enhance our information base.

The following table demonstrates some of the current understanding of distribution of body function and its expression in the brain. Additional characteristics of each side of the brain were noted in chapter one.

LEFT BRAIN	RIGHT BRAIN
Focal precise organization similar units Precise coded data organizer	Diffuse organization-dissimilar units Synthesizes unlike data Internodal and integrating
Sequential linear processing Observes and analyzes detail Organizes	Simultaneous processing and wholistic (gestalt) thinking Intuitive problem solving Spontaneity
Expressive and receptive language	Processes nonverbal stimuli Visual spatial tasks, spatial location and mental rotation Perception of body in space
Reading comprehension Letter and word recognition	
Mental and written calculation	Math reasoning and judgement
Fine motor skills Repeating movements, following commands, movement sequencing and imitation of movement controlled- habitual-restrained	Large body movements Sustaining posture and movement, Rhythm Automatic-Casual
Positive emotions and expressions	Negative emotions Perception of emotion Self expression of feeling
Stiff, rigid, restrained Marching	Loose, fluid, dance
Symmetry, systems	Shape, Shade, Movement
Close, visual organization	Distant, color
Tree	Forest

Specialization of function in various parts of the brain isolates not only right and left brain but also front and back of the brain as well as its higher and lower regions. The fact is that access to, and use of, the whole brain allows us to play our best golf.

One can readily appreciate the tremendously complex processes the brain performs in attempting a normal task. The brain receives a constant stream of input stimuli from multiple sources. Our central nervous system must utilize many different types of thinking and processes accessing and integrating the entire brain and nervous system. As you evaluate this complexity it would appear that the brain computer is not confined to what we dissect as the nervous system. Instead, it is a total body system of "sensory data collection units" and "motor expression tools".

Earlier in this book we took a tongue in cheek look at the golf swing. Take a look now at a golf swing with the new data you have accumulated. The following is paraphrased from an article by Mike McGetrick in *Golf for Women,* March/April 1993, pp.50-53.

> In the set up, the foot stance is not quite as wide as the shoulders. It is wide enough for stability yet narrow enough to allow for weight shift. The weight is evenly distributed between the right and left sides. The left foot is flared about a quarter turn toward the target to promote the uncoiling of the body during the down swing. The ball is played opposite the left armpit to position it at the bottom of the swing arc. Hands are set slightly ahead of the ball in position to begin one piece take away. Bend from the hips to maintain the angle of the spine. Arms are relaxed and hanging naturally from the shoulders. Knees are slightly flexed and weight is set on the balls of the feet for maximum balance. The clubface is squared to the target while feet, knees, hips, forearms, shoulders and eyes are all aligned parallel to the target line. In a one piece take away the club, hands, arms and shoulders all move together keeping the clubface square and preparing the body for the coil around the right side. The clubface is kept low to the ground as the turn begins. As the club reaches waist height the body weight shifts to the right side. The hands and club stay in front of the body to maintain the proper plane of the club. The shaft of the club is parallel to the

ground and the wrists are starting to cock. The shaft of the club points down a line parallel left to the target line. As the club reaches the top of the swing the body has coiled around the right side so that the right hip is directly above the right heel. The left shoulder is fully turned underneath the chin. The club shaft is pointing parallel left to the target line and almost perfectly horizontal. As the club starts the downswing the body shifts left and begins to uncoil. The body continues to rotate to the left to clear the way for full arm extension and release. With weight shifted left the right heel rises slightly off the ground. Now, three quarters of the way through the swing the arms are fully extended and ready to fold into the finish. The belt buckle is facing the target. Completing the balanced finish the right heel is up and the weight is fully transferred to the left. The belt buckle now points slightly to the left of the target.

In the golf swing the brain is doing focal point organization, sequential linear processing, detail observance, organization, fine motor focus, stiff, restrained, and calculated movement. These are all left brain analytical activities. The golfer must utilize the integrative function, the right brain, to synthesize the swing and simultaneously process the actions in an wholistic way. The golfer must sense where his body is, make the large body movements rhythmically and in a fluid fashion, "let go", and hit the ball. Notice how much easier your reading of the golf swing description would have been with pictures of the positions described. "By seeing a good swing analyzed in photos and words, you reinforce your mental image of proficient movement and strengthen your subconscious approach to your own swing. You see the whole separated into its parts, understand the interrelationship of those parts, and then adapt the essential fundamentals to your physical makeup." (Kehoe, p.8, Golf for Women, April 93) Further data from your own experience (called muscle memory) adds reality. Now, as you see, hear, feel the complexity and enormity of the data involved in a golf swing—you can appreciate the complex nature of data integration of input, throughput, and output to achieve the correct swing consistently. Little wonder it might get dis-integrated. Also, as complex and detailed as it is, there is no way to analyze your performance through the one-plus second golf swing. You must totally rely on the integrated brain/body to produce the swing. Gallwey and Wiren both provide an extensive discussion to educate the reader to the techniques needed to get out of the analytical mode and "flow" with the integrative mode. Gallwey recommends methods of alternate focus while Wiren/Coop talk about such things as swing cues to trigger the brain/body to affectively switch hemispheres. Comments from golfers after having received Performance Integration℠ treatment indicate that they now have coordinated access to the whole brain which produces a fluid, wholistic motion.

> The most specific thing I notice is when I stand up to hit the ball, I used to go through a mental chain of thoughts. It was a process of take the club back and take it back low. It was a complete chain. Now I seem to stand up and hit it. It has all come together. It's not a chain of thoughts, its just one motion and it has just come together for me that way.
>
> A.C. Female amateur

> The biggest difference is, again, the fluidity that I feel in my golf swing, and I am not swinging in parts. I am not as mechanical with my golf as I have been in the past. I can leave the mechanics on the practice tee and just go with the flow on the golf course.
>
> B.H. Male professional

> I feel myself more fluid in my swing and my take away.
>
> N.L. Male amateur

Golfers indicate that they are able to "let go" as described by Wiren and Coop suppressing the mechanics of the "Analyzer" and allowing the "Integrator" to put their golf swing together. This sense and experience is common following Performance Integration℠ and statements and feelings like these are evident throughout the expressed experiences of many types of athletes after they receive integration treatment.

The golf swing demonstrates the multi-tasking, multi-function and multi-level effort the brain engages in to create one complex act. Given this complexity in combination with all other brain activity it is not surprising the golfer is challenged to achieve consistency. Of course the golf swing itself is only a small piece of the entire game—the pinnacle moment; but there is a good deal of game management building up to that swing. Listen to Arnold Palmer describe the "headwork" of a golf pro.

> "The pro—watch him next time—is always thinking. He is thinking about the directions and speed of the wind, and the condition of the fairway. He is looking for the best spot to aim the ball, balancing the dangers of getting into a trap or the rough against the advantages of being in position for a nice open second shot to the green. He is always prepared to sacrifice the artistic for the practical. After all, the entire idea of golf is to get the ball in the hole in the fewest possible number of strokes. There is no point in sending a perfect pitch shot to the flag if the green won't hold; so the pro will gladly settle for a little punch shot and roll the ball on; it doesn't look as pretty but it gets the job done. He is always looking for lies and grass conditions that will permit him to use his putter rather than a chip shot when he's off the edge of the green, for there is always less danger of error with the putter."
>
> (Palmer, 1983 p.74)

At a focal moment of performance, the left brain is busy analyzing data while the right brain (integrator) incorporates the big picture—the overall view. The whole brain is used to meet a particular task or challenge.

Like the professional, these are some states we want to achieve in our golf game. When we play a round of golf we want to be: 1. In control—unruffled by circumstances of the weather, day, course, personal weaknesses, and strengths; 2. At calculated emotional distanced—away from the distraction of playing companions, lovers, etc. (recall John Daly being served a subpoena, a lawsuit by a former lover, while he was mid-practice in a tournament; they subsequently married); 3. Mission oriented—never losing sight of the goal despite setbacks of individual holes and shots, compartmentalizing all facets of your personal life and putting them all out of your conscious awareness except for this current game and; 4. Being systematic and methodical—setting up and performing every tactic and shot the same way you always have.

Is anything missing from this equation? Indeed, the ultimate golfer can be just a bit "robotic"! This may be an appropriate term to describe that analytical, linear thinking, critical, judgmental, controlled, habitual, restrained, stiff, rigid, organized left brained individual. The reader can appreciate here some difficulty in discussing human performance and in reality finding that there isn't any behavior or action that is fully left or right brained.

Timothy Gallwey in his book *The Inner Game of Golf* (1979) does not use the model of hemispheric specialization that analyzes roles of separate portions of the brain. He views the brain as the home of two "selves" of the same personality. Self-1 is portrayed more as a saboteur or compulsive controller while Self-2 becomes the true whole person, expressed as permitted by Self-1. The model is useful. Creating models of this brain/body system has been difficult since so little is known about it. Perhaps we could characterize Self-1 as always focused, poised, and ready to analyze. Self-2 would be effortlessly flowing and harmonious with the universe, simply the product of letting go and functioning on automatic pilot. The Self-1 and Self-2 model can be useful to help us integrate our notions of what is actually taking place inter-brain/intra-brain and brain/body. Self-1 would be the objective, conscious, mental effort, while Self-2 would be instinctive reaction. Gallwey states, "both right and left hemispheres are part of the human body. I look at Self-2 (the integrator) as the total human organism, the natural entity. Self-1 (the analyzer), on the other hand, does not actually have a physical existence; he is a phenomenon of mental self-interference who can and does interfere with both right-and left-hemisphere functions. Self-doubt, for example, can be as crippling in a mathematics test as in a tennis match, on a golf course or in singing a song. But when the mind is concentrated and absorbed in what it is doing, interference is minimized and the brain is able to function closer to its potential.

When Self-1 and Self-2 are clearly defined in this way, the basic premise of the Inner Game can be expressed in a simple equation. The quality of our performance relative to our actual potential is equal to our potential (Self-2) minus the interference with the expression of that potential (Self-1). Or: Performance=Self-2 (potential) minus Self-1 (interference).

"Thus, the aim of the Inner Game is not so much to try harder to persuade Self-2 to do what he is capable of doing, but to decrease the Self-1 interferences that prevent Self-2 from expressing himself fully." (p.4)

No one is only left brained. For good or ill there are right brain or whole brain characteristics evident in all our behaviors. Whether our mission is a good round of golf or a successful business negotiation, balance is the key to the whole personality and its expressions. Balance is critical to the full life. Gratefully, this balance is often a life saver. Our relationships, businesses, etc, might not survive some of those singular devastating moments of loss of balance. One can focus with the singular left brained exasperation of relentless, rigid and critical analysis on a failed golf shot or lighten up and with the wholistic (gestalt) right brain view golf as a part of a whole and balanced life.

We mentioned earlier four states of "being" that were desirable in our golf game. They were 1. In control, 2. At calculated emotional distance, 3. Mission oriented, and 4. Systematic and methodical. Various research, including my own (Kennedy and Porter, 1989) discusses this phenomenon in military aviators. These flyers are highly trained and capable. They assume these states of being in preparation for military missions. Part of the "head work" they use under stress is called "compartmentalization". In this process they prioritize action and relegate brain activity to compartments. Activities and thoughts not pertinent are put on hold. This compartmentalization is the creation of walls in the mind to block out other functions or experience or memory that might divert or distract the aviator from the completion of his mission. The notion of compartmentalization has value to the golfer. The necessity of this useful tool is evident as Arnold Palmer (1983) discusses the low physical tension of the golf game which doesn't give you repeated physical contact or effort to "blow off" the last negative experience you've had. He says: "In golf there are no safety valves at all. You're under pressure; you're under tension; in a tournament you can feel the crowd's excitement and tension, which add to your own. Yet you have to execute every shot in cold blood, so to speak. You have to force yourself, each time you address the ball, to be calm and cool and detached, like a surgeon wielding a scalpel." (p.55). Whether a tour pro or a weekend golfer, we all carry our inner "crowds" with us which distract our attention along with all the other sensory inputs of our bodies. Compartmentalization can be a valuable skill for diminishing and controlling outside influences on our golf game. Those distractions include emotions and the unpredictability of the course as well as our own game's unpredictability.

Compartmentalization is under more deliberate control in the integrated brain. The experiences of athletes receiving Performance Integration[SM] suggest that they more easily control their transitions from Analyzer to Integrator. Also, they are more readily able to stop the analytical "trying" and get on with the integrative "doing".

Now that we've discussed "hemispheric specialization" in aviators and golfers, look at these interesting excerpts from the post integration treatment testimonial of J.G. He is an airline pilot, and piloted an RF-4 reconnaissance jet in the recent Gulf War. This is your well-trained, peak performance aviator. The following is his testimony regarding the correction of his neurologic dis-integration:

> It has been a valuable experience. I have learned to accommodate certain features of my body in ways that I haven't been able to do before or even recognize the ability to do before. I found it very valuable in terms of flying an airplane, to be able to assimilate greater amounts of information more rapidly, and to be able to make decisions more quickly with that information at hand.
>
> I have found that the treatment has provided me with the ability to look at the instrument panel in a single glance and assimilate information that formerly required several scans of the instrument panel over a period of time. It has been a very valuable experience having come back from a war to realize that not only the training but this new ability that I have gained through this treatment has provided me with the opportunity to enjoy flying more and to be more proficient at flying. (Interview, Spring 1992)

This pilot is now more aware of his sensory information. He is using it more effectively giving him greater skill as well as enjoyment. What's good for the aviator is good for the golfer! One professional golfer who received Performance Integration℠ treatment noticed positive changes in his golf game, but was more impressed by two other occurrences. First, after a multi-year lay off from tennis playing, which was not a primary sport for him, he was "extremely surprised" at how well he played. His tennis skill was beyond his normal expectation after the long lay off. And second, to his and his wife's delight, his performance on the dance floor was remarkably improved.

What happened to this golfer's tennis and dancing abilities was virtually the release of the "paralysis of analysis" of the left brain allowing the integration of his performance by the right brain. This reminds us of our golf instructor saying, "Now just put this whole swing together and let it happen". Proper neurologic integration greatly enhances our ability to draw upon the whole self in function and to do so more freely. The transcripts of complete post integration testimonials in the appendix will help you get a sense of other life enhancing affects of neurologic integration.

You can see that this very complex computer and its body output are better understood as we understand hemispheric specialization, lateralization, and compartmentalization.

Let's use the computer model of data processing to further understand the phenomenon of neurologic integration. Neurology teaches us that in lower level brain processes other important operations are occurring. As humans, we generally use the same basic operating systems in our central processing units, the brain, and its extensions. Generally, without disease or abnormal chemical contamination of the brain, we all operate pretty much alike. Remember, we do our own data collection. That data in our somewhat generic brain is processed through some apparently standard processes that differ only a little from individual to individual. If two people had exactly the same experience and data collection, they would still process that data in different ways to perform a math problem, or other activity. Cochran and Stobbs (1968) said this about the illusive "perfect" golf swing, "No man, of course, has achieved, or ever will achieve, the absolutely perfect swing. If he did, his golf would be infallible—at least up to the greens! But the length of time for which golf has been played, and the very many variations in style which have been tried, together suggest that the methods used by the most successful players are likely to come pretty close to the best method possible: allowing, of course, for all those individual variations of physique, muscle structure, suppleness and—not least important—temperament, which together prevent everybody ending up with precisely the same swing."(p.8)

The beauty and complexity of individuals is enhanced by the fact that no two people can have the same experience even with the same data. Styles of processing probably differ a great deal, and for good reason. An illustration of difference in processing styles might be the instance of a man and wife planning a trip. Commonly, spouses have quite different approaches to planning, preparation, concerns, schedules, expectations, to accomplish a simple weekend getaway. Rarely do two people arrive at similar conclusions without considerable exchange of data and its evaluation. A good measure of communication and work is required.

The key point is this: with the same basic hardware, we all do our own data collection and processing. Individuals, like snowflakes, are very unique. This explains why neurologic disintegration manifests itself in numerous ways. Likewise, neurologic integration obtains a variety of different results. As you will learn in Chapter 9, general end products of neurologic integration fall into categories of performance that reflect a commonality of the basics of self-realization. That is, if we are all integrated, we may all obtain the ability to organize, ability to concentrate, enhanced self-esteem, self-control, self-confidence, and learning ability that we discussed earlier.

We cannot create a model that would have us all processing data the same way, thus creating the same consistent outcomes. It is logical that our basic operating systems use similar data processing technology. In his article "The Cognitive Revolution and Mind/Brain Issues" (May 1986) Karl Pribram of Standford University said, "computers and their programs provide a useful metaphor in the analysis of the mind/brain issue in which the distinction between brain, mind and spirit can be seen as similar to the distinction between machine (hardware), low level programs (e.g. operating systems), and high level programs (e.g. word processing programs)" (Pribram p.509).

These comments reiterate the postulate that primary survival level programs may operate similarly in all human beings. Higher level processes may take on a more personal, and certainly more sophisticated nature. The lower levels perform basic operations while the higher levels process data. And further, "The essence of biological as well as of computational hierarchies is that higher levels of organization take control over, as well as being controlled by, lower levels." (Ibid p.509) An understanding of this basic structure and its form of operation lets us appreciate why neurologic dis-organization/organization creates the performance we see in golf and other human endeavors. Thus, in whole brain activity, primal instinct may suggest that deliberate subtle suggestions about your golf performance might rattle you enough to cause you to duff the shot. Meanwhile your higher brain/right brain holistic view would override this with the notion that it's only a game and may the best man win. The sophistication and enjoyment of our golf experience may well reflect the operative level of our brain. How we conduct ourselves on the course, whether alone or with companions, speaks of our own level of evolution neurologically, mentally, and emotionally. Ouch! (Tip. The key to breaking into warp speed and attaining the highest levels of evolutionary progress on the golf course is most likely learning to laugh at oneself.) The components of this postulate are discussed thoroughly in Chapter 9, Performance Integration℠ Theory.

The suggestion is that lower levels of brain function (survival level functions) interplay with the higher "thinking" levels of the brain. This interplay provides the basis for the techniques of manipulation that we use in mental games with ourselves and with others. We may use our intellectual word processing programs to trigger our or another's survival level programs, such as those regarding security, well-being, and the like. This pulls us into the stress reaction survival "fight/flight" mode. This is our anxiety reaction and can include the clenched teeth and tight muscles that fouled up our last game of golf. Neurologic integration does not eliminate natural anxiety reflexes but our clinical research indicates that it greatly reduces the incidence of stress reactions in the individual. In other words, *the integrated nervous system is able to exercise greater control over stress reaction in the body.* This appears to be a secondary benefit of processing data and assessing "life", golf, business, or anything. Integrated, we use the whole brain, thus the broad based benefits of neurologic integration. The following chapter looks at the outcomes of Performance Integration^{SM} procedures.

CHAPTER 5

GOLF BETTER AUTOMATICALLY

INTEGRATION RESULTS

What happens when hemispheric integration and lateralization function suboptimally in the golfer? Let's look at information from the literature on the subject and correlate it with the post-Performance Integration^{SM} changes noted by several golfers. After golfers receive Performance Integration^{SM} protocol, there is a very explicit and demonstrable change in Applied Kinesiology tests. This is changed motor behavior. Muscles that were weak now test strong. This suggests a change in brain data processing due to improved integration. In other words, their body parts act more coordinated and more under control of the brain. Brain and body are communicating better. After treatment, golfers talk about changes in their mental/emotional life further suggesting integration. The Applied Kinesiology testing method is very reliable in the hands of a practiced technician. The changes are immediate and completely apparent to the treated person. Athletes tested noticed that many of their muscles would not crisply lock as expected before integration. Directly after integration, they saw that their muscles were normally responsive just like the other muscles of their bodies. Beyond these changes of muscle test are the personal case reports of the treated person. Because some of the changes are subjective, they are not easily submitted to the strict research ideology of "science". This is as it should be. Why?

Remember that we all program our own computer. Therefore we must all anticipate different effects when our brain begins to function more efficiently. The objective change in the muscle test is a consistently reproducible phenomenon. The self-actualization or mental/physical output changes of the body, including attitudes and beliefs, vary from individual to individual.

Both the change in motor output and that of self-actualization behavior combine to provide a decided change in performance which gives one "the edge". That edge in athletics will be obvious as you read the upcoming golfers' experiences. The change is of course personal, and spills over into all the golfer's activities. The *integrated individual is different* than the dis-integrated individual. Case reports testify that an edge, or advantage may be gained in many areas of human performance. Research and study of Performance Integration^{SM} has consistently been done using individuals who were already peak performers. This is done for two reasons. First, they *recognize performance change* in themselves because they frequently give attention or awareness to their performance levels. Second, they are *result oriented* and can be expected to be analytical and critical about their results. This discussion of integration results is only a small part of the total collected data and experience contained in the sections of this book. See the appendix for a few complete interviews. The purpose of it is to clearly demonstrate how the individual hemispheres of the brain are directly affected by, and responsive to, Performance Integration℠. The evidence overwhelmingly shows that wholistic brain functioning (i.e., right and left, up and down, front and back communication in the brain) is taking place more efficiently after integration. The golfers' physical actions and subjective experiences tell us that more of their computer is available to process data.

These findings are discussed in a somewhat orderly fashion in deference to our left brain listing mode. As a golfer on the tee, in the rough, or playing out of a bunker, the challenge of organizing data includes, but is not limited to, consideration of player ability, lie of the ball, character of the ground, shot options, weather, relation of location to destination, club availability, level of motivation, worth of the shot, and more. Putting this list of data together is a right brain function. Neurologic dis-organization causes difficulty with processing information in this wholistic way and prevents the brain from seeing the big picture. It prevents viewing, weighing and properly synthesizing all the data. Following Performance Integration℠ treatment golfers reported better organization and prioritization by the brain/body.

One golfer commented: "I am starting to think better. I am thinking my way through a golf course now rather than just hitting the golf ball. And that's making a lot of difference in the way I play golf, which really has had a big affect on even how I approach certain holes."   J.M. Male amateur

Another golfer talking about the biggest difference in his golf game since Performance Integration℠ said: "It's organization, pure and simple. I take all aspects of the hole into consideration. In fact, when I played the tournament at Squaw

Creek, before I went out on the course, I took an extra ten minutes by myself. When I was out on the practice tee I thought about a number of holes in the golf course I already knew that were real tough to play and how I would play them when I play them. When I got there I was just ready to play the hole as if it was any other hole in the golf course and not especially the toughest one for my style of game.

I don't tend to move the ball in big sways from right to left or left to right. I draw the ball and I fade the ball, but I am not a hooker at all. And some of the holes on that particular golf course you have definitely got to either hook or fade the ball. I found myself more able just to approach the hole and play it much better than I had in the past. I just know there's a big difference, and I am more relaxed."

N.L. Male amateur

Emotional stability and staying on course are right hemisphere functions. Discomfort in new situations and around unfamiliar people is an indicator of reduced integration. This sensitivity can affect the golfer's focus, drawing attention away from play. This would be particularly critical in tournament play or under pressure that comes from playing with strangers. Dis-organization disperses the player's attention. The golfer is unable to most effectively compartmentalize effort and drive the self to absolute attention to the game at hand. Other thoughts and feelings compete for attention, robbing the golfer of clear, undisturbed focus on play. Integrated golfers indicated that they have both enhanced confidence and greater control.

"The control comes, for me, in keeping in tempo. And because I have maintained better patience and tempo during a round, I am hitting a lot more fairways and a lot more greens through the round and that gives you confidence."

M.M. Male professional

"When I stand over the ball for the short game, I just have a real feeling of knowing what I want to do with the club. Where as before (Integration) there were times I stood there and ask which option do I want? Now, I feel like the option is right there in the front of my mind. That should definitely take off some strokes on the game."

J.U. Female professional

"I guess the thing that I have noticed is more of a mellowness that I have had, more of a feeling that things are just happening because I am a little bit more in control of my feelings, a little bit more in control in my game when it comes to golf, and a little bit more in control of my life."

R.C. Male amateur

"I just think it has probably made me a little more low key, laid back, and I don't worry about it as much. This relaxes me in golf. You have to be relaxed in golf. You've got to quit worrying about everything and just get up there and strike the ball. I think that has helped me a lot."

B.A. Male amateur

Visual and spatial organization are functions of the right brain hemisphere. Though more commonly appreciated in drawing or handwriting, the manifestation of this dis-integration difficulty is in getting the hand to perform in smooth, flowing fashion. This function relates to control of tools, including golf clubs. Handling tools effectively involves the ability to input sensory data through the eye, hand, and body, then process the data with unbroken communication causing the hand to perform as commanded by the brain. Fine tuning of where the body is in relation to itself is a phenomena of mental self-perception or self-location that is right hemisphere controlled. My own earlier research with naval aviators corroborates the findings in our study of golfers.

Research with 20 US Navy pilots and crew members before and after Performance Integration^{SM} procedures produced interesting results. These men were tested pre- and post-integration with the micro-computer based Automated Performance Test System©. The following statement is from the data analysis:

"The Manikin test is probably the most interesting. This perceptual rotation cognitive test measures spatial abilities and is one of the more difficult tests in the battery....the subjects in this study did not stabilize but continued to improve markedly. This may be the most relevant tasks for pilots since it logically should relate to spatial orientation." (Kennedy and Porter, 1989 p.8)

In this test the aviators looked at a manikin figure on a computer screen and were able to interpret its relative rotational position faster and more accurately than others taking the test who were not treated. They were interpreting data more quickly indicating improved communication and processing between right and left brain. This ability is critical to the aviator who, in a rapidly changing positional environment of jet aircraft maneuvers, must constantly be able to locate his relative position. Integration improved this crucial and vital ability by enhancing brain/body communication.

This "sense of body placement relative to environment" is called proprioception and is reliant on data processed in the brain from the eyes, inner ears, and body parts. The improved proprioception data processing, input to output, is perceived and expressed by integrated golfers as better coordination. It's you and all of your environment relative to you. Comments made by integrated golfers which support this include:

> I think the biggest part of my golf game was improved through my timing and my coordination.
>
> S.W. Female amateur

> I have been better balanced. I am swinging with proper mechanics now. I am not manipulating the club with the hand and arms to produce the shots I want; and consequently, it's much easier to manage a game because you know how far your clubs are going to go. G.R. Male professional

> Since integration, I am more coordinated, I would say it's probably 10 to 15 percent. ...being an athlete, I feel that I am pretty coordinated to begin with. So that is pretty significant.
>
> A.W. Male professional

In the same research with the naval aviators noted above, there was marked improvement in eye-hand coordination response and short term memory. All three of these items were objectively measured. An informative list of their subjective experiences is included in chapter 9.

Sustaining movement and posture are phenomena of the right

hemisphere. The left brain is more associated with specificity of movement while the right brain is concerned with flow of movement. The left is deliberate while the right is automatic. After Performance Integration℠ golfers have made these observations which indicate better communication between the left and right brain hemispheres.

> I played a lot of golf in that time and found, again, a common balance between both sides. So, I wasn't dominant in one hand or the other or one leg or the other. So naturally, the ball started going much straighter because I was a more balanced swinger of the golf club. R.T. Male amateur

> In the case of golf, I felt that my whole body knew what I wanted to do rather than trying to gather all of my muscular forces together in driving off the tee and being able to keep it straight or being able to know what was going to happen. I mean in teeing off, I hope something happens after I swing back and start to swing into the ball. I think that is sort of a blind spot and then, hopefully, it works. But I did feel that I was able to manipulate my body a lot better after integration. B.G. Male amateur

The left brain hemisphere handles work, including information processing and gross motor coordination. It processes information in a sequential linear fashion and is more attentive to observation and analysis of detail. The right brain hemisphere is more adept at simultaneous processing and wholistic thinking. It solves problems more interactively, dealing with multiple alternatives at one time. The importance of integrated access to and use of both brain hemispheres is obvious.

The left brain is also primarily affective in skills involving gross motor coordination. This includes most competitive sports and dancing as distinguished from "flow and rhythm" which is more a right brain function. Applied Kinesiology testing demonstrates that the neurologically dis-organized athlete has gaps in the flow patterns of athletic performance sequences. You may be familiar with the fact that the brain/body can visualize athletic sequences and events mentally without actually performing them. This technique is used by athletes to practice or prepare themselves for performance. Electrical studies of muscle activity have revealed that the muscles do respond as if truly in action when this mental review is occurring. Now with Applied Kinesiology we are able to evaluate the congruity and continuity of this mental/physical phenomenon. In mental or physical action the golfer's swing can be analyzed by testing a strong muscle. Without exception, this testing has revealed incongruity and discontinuity in the golf swing of dis-integrated golfers. There are parts of their golf swings which are not consistently under control of the whole brain.

These gaps in brain/body communication suppress optimal function. Post integration testing consistently demonstrates that brain/body communication gaps are correctable. Post integration reports of golfers suggest that their left brain motor coordination has teamed up with their right brain flow and rhythm.

> Again, I think it was coordination. It seemed I would hit a bad golf shot, and I could feel it in my swing. I am able to groove my swing more consistently than I was before. The bad shots still come, but not as frequently, and it seems that the swing is much more consistent than before. I am more coordinated. Less concentration required to get the swing is the feeling I have. The swing, whether it's the tee shots, whether it's the long game or the short game, I can keep the swing the same tempo and the same rhythm which I wasn't able to do before. You know when you can do things consistently, then the golf ball is going to go the right way. Since then (integration) I have been able to do that. It's more coordinated effort without the intense concentration that I thought was required to make myself do it. It's easier, smoother, and more coordinated, I feel. K.G. Male amateur

This general statement can be made regarding left brain integration and training activities. These expressed abilities and functions of the left hemisphere are fundamental to one's ability to be trained easily in a motor skill, particularly a gross motor skill such as golf. The player's ability to reproduce the important directions of the golf pro are very much left hemispheric. Interestingly, the pro will instruct the left brain and the pupil will reproduce the activity from the left brain. The pro will then talk about feeling how it all feels. The pro is moving the pupil from the sequential, linear, analytical, and detailed left brain performance to the affective right brain by saying, "Feel how it feels". What the pro is seeking is to have the golfer synthesize this pattern and experience with their right brain and, thus, create an wholistic, flowing action.

What the Performance Integration℠ did for me was clear up the confusion that I had on my own swing. As a teacher I am able to communicate swing thoughts and feelings better and in a more coherent manner to my students. It allowed me to create a stronger communication base. I understood the motion better. I had been working on about four or five different things when I first became integrated, and everything just shortly thereafter cleared up and fell into place.

G.R. Male professional

I had taken golf lessons before, several years ago, when I tried to take the game up at that time. This time there was a major difference and the major difference specifically was in the mental process of the game. Although, I am hitting much better too. I feel that I am able to visualize a lot better than I have ever been able to do. I am able to take the time in the setup and focus, and focus has been a general overall problem in my life before. So, I feel it's mostly mental with me because it's not fair to say the physical part improved a lot because I am just starting again. D.H. Female amateur

This experience makes sense. Understanding the theory and outcomes of integration contributes to better understanding of the practical and the mental sides of golf. Unveiling the mystery of how the brain/body works we are better able to utilize the tools we have.

You can see now how the physical and mental sides of golfing may not be integrated, causing some of the inconsistencies in your golf game. Although these explanations are somewhat simplistic they help us understand why peak performance is so elusive. Our complex systems perform remarkably well despite neurologic disorganization.

CHAPTER 6

ACCESSING YOUR GOLF COMPUTER PROGRAM

APPLIED KINESIOLOGY

Applied Kinesiology is a system that is unique in the healing arts. Officially introduced in 1964 by Dr. George Goodheart D.C. "It is the art of isolating and testing a single muscle to determine if it is weak or strong relative to the strength of the individual being tested "(Dennison p. 16). "Most muscle tests done in Applied Kinesiology do not evaluate the power a muscle can produce; rather they evaluate how the nervous system controls muscle function. This has been called muscle testing as functional neurology"(Walther p.2). Although practitioners refer to the tested muscle as "weak" or "strong", it is important to note that physical strength is not what is being measured. The concern is whether the muscle *functions* properly at the command of the individual. Testing of a muscle that is apparently and ordinarily normal in use and appearance is done to determine if it functions or acts as expected. Under the circumstances of testing by an Applied Kinesiologist, if a muscle tests "weak" when it appears and is expected to be normal, it may indicate a communication error in the body. That is, the Kinesiologist commands the individual to lock a muscle in strength against the pressure of his test. If the muscle can't hold or lock, it is acting as if it doesn't get the message from the tested person's brain. There is therefore a communication error between the brain and that muscle. The concept of communication disruption in the body is very important. The cause of dis-organization in body function or neurology is communication disruption or improper signaling. If you command your muscle to be strong against the test of the kinesiologist and it is not strong- then the muscle is not getting the message. There is a communication disorder in which the nerve signals in your body are being mishandled or are improperly functioning.

The weakness is a diagnostic indicator which leads the Kinesiologist to a causative factor. When the improper function is corrected the weakness disappears. The muscle will then test consistently strong as expected for a normal (integrated) person.

Dr. Goodheart states, "Applied Kinesiology is based on the fact that the body language never lies. The opportunity for understanding the body language is enhanced by the ability to use muscles as indicators of body language. Once muscle weakness has been ascertained a variety of therapeutic options is available. The opportunity to use the body as an instrument of laboratory analysis is unparalleled in modern therapeutics because the response of the body is unerring" (Dennison, p.29).

Study of the muscles found weak in the dis-integrated golfer lead us to understand many of the inconsistencies of golf performance. Further, correction of the cause of these weaknesses improves golf performance.

CHAPTER 7

RELEASING THE GOLFER WITHIN

FULL BODY GOLF

The hallmark of neurologic dis-organization is a pattern in the individual of sub-optimal muscle response. Muscles actually perform in a weakened fashion. How does that affect the golf swing? In their book, *The Search for the Perfect Swing,* Cochran and Stobbs note: "All of the muscles are singly and jointly controlled by coordinated electrical impulses sent down nerves from the brain, and they also send back continuous and equally highly coordinated information to the brain describing their position and state of tension at any moment. Singly and together they thus function as a highly coordinated, versatile and delicately controlled engine to produce force and power (p.80).

"One other characteristic of the muscles is relevant. The power they give depends on the speed at which they are able to contract (react, respond). In general, big muscles work at their greatest efficiency, and thus give their greatest power, when working comparatively slowly; whereas small muscles give their peak performance when moving fast"(Ibid).

In the *integrated golfer*, muscles react quickly and exactly, on demand. This is the essential element of the argument for integration of the responses of the muscles. Dis-integration inhibits, discoordinates and slows the muscle responses of the body.

Look at the overall mechanics of the golf swing and the potential effects of neurologic disorganization on that golf swing. I will discuss those muscles which most commonly are found weak in the dis-organized individual. I will identify the muscle, tell you its function, and why it is important to the golf swing. Refer to the illustration to locate these muscles. I will refer to the definitive work of Jobe, et al(1989,1990), to help you understand upper body muscle function. You will see the connections between neurologic integration, the weak muscles of disorganization, and your golf swing. Jobe's work was initiated in order to understand the mechanics of the swing well enough to understand golfers' injuries. He also prescribes proper exercise for conditioning the golfer in his book *30 Exercises for Better Golf* (1986). His studies included eight muscles of the upper body and shoulder area. Of these eight, three are commonly found weak in the neurologically dis-organized individual. They are the latissimus dorsi (usually the right is weak), the pectoralis major (usually the left one is weak), and the middle deltoid (right or left is weak in approximately equal incidence).

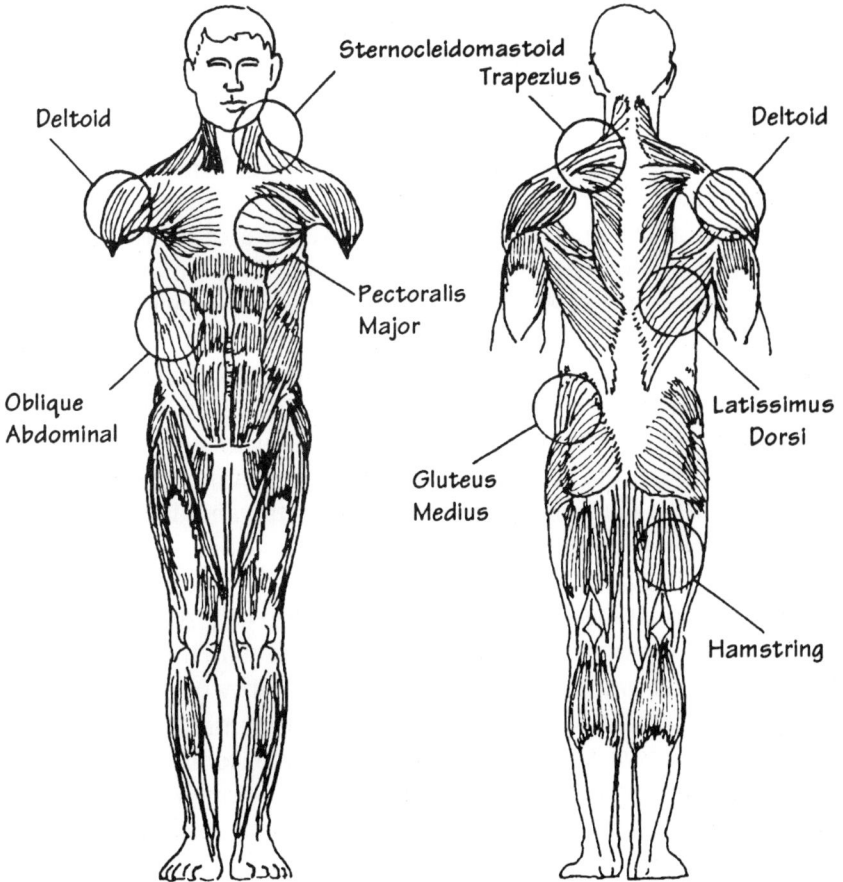

Deltoid

Sternocleidomastoid
Trapezius

Deltoid

Pectoralis
Major

Oblique
Abdominal

Latissimus
Dorsi

Gluteus
Medius

Hamstring

Action of the pectoralis major is to pull the shoulder joint down and to pull the humerus into the body. Jobe stated "The right pectoralis major has significantly more activity during forward swing, acceleration, and early follow through...Acceleration has significantly more activity than did late follow through. In the left pectoralis major there was significantly more activity during acceleration than during take away and forward swing."(Jobe,et al,1990 p.138) Action of the latissimus dorsi is to pull the arm backward (extension), to pull the humerus toward the body, and rotate it, and to pull the shoulder blade down and in. Jobe noted that "The right latissimus dorsi had significantly more activity during forward swing and acceleration. In the left latissimus dorsi there was more activity,...during forward swing than during any of the other phases".(Ibid)

Action of the middle deltoid is to lift the arm away from the body. Jobe found "No significant differences in the middle deltoid for the right or left sides. There were low levels of activity for all phases"(Ibid p.139) of the golf swing. Anterior and posterior deltoid muscles were tested by Jobe and found to contribute little activity in the golf swing. These two muscles variously test weak in the right or left shoulder of the neurologically dis-organized person. Though the deltoid is not significant in the golf swing, it is important to the balance and stability of the shoulder joint and its movements. In addition, Jobe's testing revealed no significant difference between men and women in the muscles tested. Functions stayed the same although men were 40% stronger.

One muscle of the upper body and trunk which has not been tested in the laboratory but is weak in the majority of the neurologically dis-organized is the external oblique abdominal. The action of this muscle is to flex the spine forward, help stabilize the anterior pelvis, and to rotate the spine bringing the shoulder forward on the same side. It is active in the forward swing and acceleration phase of the golf swing. It contributes to stability and balance in the full swing. The abdominals are critical in that they tie the top of the torso to the pelvis making them a dominant connecting link between the golf swing of the upper body and the powerful torquing of the lower body. While upper chest and back muscles pull the arms down and up creating a twist around the hub of the head and neck, the abdominals combine pelvic turn with upper body turn.

Your own experience has taught you that those few muscles discussed in the upper body are indeed not the whole story. You've probably been sore in a lot of muscles we didn't mention after the first two buckets of balls at the beginning of a new season.

Analysis by Cochran and Stobbs concluded that the golf swing generates three to four horse power and the "power available from the arms amounts at most to one and a quarter horse power"(p.81). The large lower body muscles generate the approximately two and a half remaining horse power. "Thus, without even considering the detailed movements in a golf swing, we can make a fundamental and far reaching statement about it: that the muscles of the legs and hips constitute the main source of power in long driving"(p.81).

These specific muscles of the lower body affect power, rhythm, timing and balance of the golf swing. Most muscles of the body are somehow participants in the golf swing. Here are two in the lower body which consistently test weak in the neurologically dis-organized individual. The first is gluteus medius which acts to pull the thigh to the body and to rotate it in. It is a major lateral pelvic stabilizer. In this role it supports the action of the lateral pelvic slide of the golf swing, participating in the timing and balance of that move. Its improper function can adversely affect the weight shift of the swing as well as its power. The second is the hamstring which flexes and internally rotates the knee, lifts the thigh back and away, and rotates it internally. This muscle is particularly important in the rotation of the hips in the swing and in stabilizing the knees. The power, timing and integration of the hamstring are significant contributors to the golf swing.

Recall the key element of "muscle weakness" which we are discussing. The muscle is not weak in the sense of not having strength; instead the muscle does not react in appropriate time and sequence to messages from the brain. In his book *The Inner Game of Golf,* Gallwey refers to overtightness of muscles as the primary cause of physical error in golf. He includes the definition of strength as the amount of weight a contracted muscle can support while "power is the ability to use strength, and requires a very sophisticated cooperative *(integrated)* effort between contracting and relaxing muscles". (p.31, italics added)

Gallwey further notes that overtightness occurs in various ways, to include overtightness of too many muscles, as in the wrist. Also, muscles of the back swing may not release for the forward swing. Muscles may tighten or contract with improper timing, such that the proper sequence of relaxation and contraction does not occur. Most of the subtler errors in the golf swing can likewise be traced to overtightness in certain parts of the body.

"But to attempt to remedy the problem by analyzing each instance of overtightness would be exasperating and self-defeating. Literally thousands of muscle units are involved in the golf swing; their timing and coordination are exquisitely precise, and are simply not accessible to intellectual understanding of Self-1 *(left brain- analytical)* control. The body coordinates these muscles in response to our general command to produce accuracy and power, but only when the execution of those goals is entrusted to it. The best conscious effort we can make is to be clear about our goal, and to keep from interfering with its execution." (Ibid, p.32, italics added)

Undeniably, any golf swing is a complex act, beyond real time self-analysis. Yes, relaxing and letting go of the well-practiced swing usually alone can improve it. Critical to your understanding is the interpretation of the many testimonials of amateur and professional golfers after they have received Performance Integration[SM] treatment. Without any effort they begin to perform the golf swing in a more relaxed and fluid manner, consistently. This suggests that the neurologically dis-organized brain/body does not control all the muscles of the body in a coordinated synchronized fashion, and the integrated brain/body does. Not that the ability to "stop analyzing and start letting go" isn't an issue in any golf swing, but in the integrated golfer, this occurs more easily, consistently, and dependably.

This occurrence of overtight muscles is also positive evidence supporting the findings that the dis-organized brain/body is locked in a stress–anxiety–fight/flight reflex. Overtight muscles and inability to relax are indicative of a stress- anxiety reflex.

The post integration reports of several athletes show us

changes which tell us that their muscles are functioning with better timing, power, and consistency.

Where it has helped me, literally, is on my mid-iron shots and off the tee because there is a big difference between hitting a four iron into the green and a six iron into the green. And now, off the tee, I am hitting the ball far enough that I am not using long irons. I am using mid-range irons or shorter irons.

J.M. male amateur

Actually, my golf game didn't really pick up until recently. I noticed my stamina increased right off. I ride bicycles also and I noticed that right off I could ride harder and faster than I ever could before. That's what I noticed first. And just recently, my golf game has been picking up...

B.A. male amateur

I started throwing the ball further when I went out with the dogs in the evenings. And when I threw the ball, it seemed like I had more control and I had more power in throwing the ball. It was just going farther than what it usually had gone. I felt more strength in my arms. K.W. female professional

I noticed some changes when some other people actually said I was making a bigger turn, and I though about it. And I was making the shoulder and the hip turn, which professionals have been trying to get me to do for 20 years, and I had not been able to do it. I don't know why, but I am the classic swayer. I sway away from it and I sway into it. Now I am turning, and I am hitting the ball just unbelievably well.

J.W. male amateur

In Las Vegas, which is considerably lower altitudewise than Reno, your ball tends not to carry as far. I am using the same club that I would at high altitude there and it's working. So, I am half a club longer on my irons.

As far as my tee shots go, I am consistently longer. 10, 12, 15 yards, but that's one club. On a long par four, I played at the resort at Squaw Creek the other day, and there's a 484 yard, par four, and I hit a driver and a four iron and it was no struggle at all. Six months ago, no chance.

N.L. male amateur

Regarding other athletic performances:

In softball, the biggest thing I notice is my legs. I just feel stronger. I feel like I am a step faster.

B.P. male professional

But from the performance side, the physical performance side, there was another surprise, and that was the weight lifting aspect, which I do every day and have for 25 years. It takes months to move a percent to move up two pounds or three pounds. I was able to move five, six to ten percent in various lifts in a matter of about a five or six week period. I sensed the difference from being able to balance and being able to lift equally with both sides of the body and being able to get centered. It was absolutely phenomenal.   R.T. male amateur

I am very active in sports and athletics. Integration really has improved my endurance in bike riding. In fact, I have a friend I could never keep up with in bike riding. Not only can I keep up with him, I won a friendly race, and that really is something I enjoyed.

Also, skiing. I noticed I have a lot more mobility and confidence in my turning whether it's a left turn or a right turn. Before, I was a little shaky with my right turns. Now, I am fully dextrous in both turns.   D.D. male athlete

I have more balance in my aerobics classes. I teach aerobics, and it was like day and night. All I did was get better and better and better. I have a problem with my left side, or, I had a problem. I had to think about what I was doing on my left side. My right side came natural to me. I'll remember it forever. I remember taking the class and teaching it, and all of a sudden, I was working on my left side, and I didn't think about it.   A.D. female athlete

After one of the later treatments I went out for a training run. My legs did not necessarily feel stronger, but I had much more contact with them than ever before. It seemed like I could have more efficient access to their strength. These new feelings have lasted the months since that treatment.

T.K. male amateur

CHAPTER 8

BRAIN/BODY TEAMWORK

WHAT'S WRONG WITH THE DIS-ORGANIZED GOLFER?

In a healthy individual, muscles function in a predictable way. The predictable behavior of a person tested standing in a neutral position or lying on an examining table in a neutral position, is that all muscles when individually tested will test strong on the normal neurologically integrated person. Under ordinary circumstances when a person is moving through space, some muscles test strong (turned on) while other muscles test weak (turned off). For example, when we walk we place one leg forward and the opposite arm forward while their opposites move back. That is, right arm and left leg go forward while left arm and right leg go back. The brain controls this activity by stimulating the flexor or forward pulling muscles of the leg and arm moving forward and inhibiting the flexor muscles of the opposite arm and leg so the muscles on the back sides, or extensors, can pull those limbs back. With each subsequent step, of course, the reverse action occurs, so that opposite arm and leg flexors are stimulated while their opposite flexors are inhibited. In this way, we create a coordinated turning on and turning off of muscles to allow proper gait to occur.

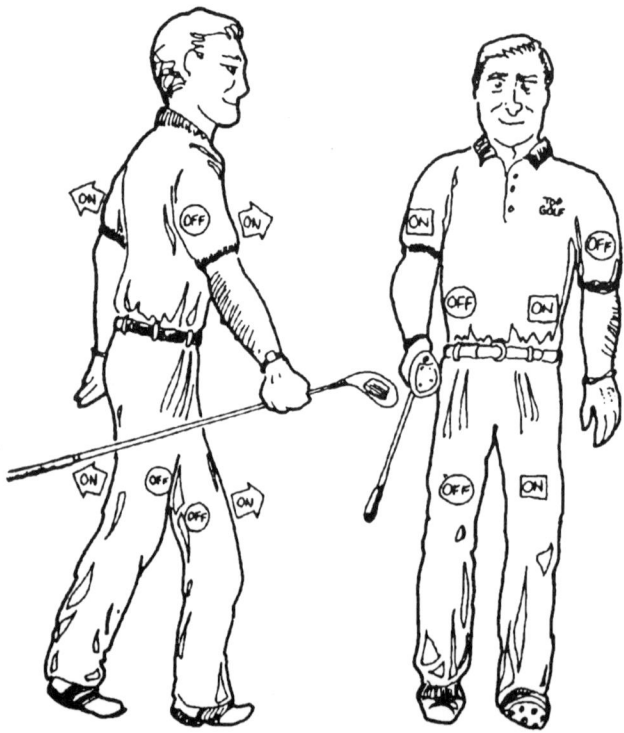

Under normal conditions, muscle tests will reveal that, in the normal individual, muscles that are supposed to be stimulated or turned on will test *strong*. Their opposites, which are supposed to be inhibited or turned off, will test weak. This is what we expect in the normal healthy individual. In the neurologically dis-organized person, these tests will *not* produce results consistent with the expected behavior. Muscles that should be weak may test strong and vice versa. Thus, there is a confusion in the nervous system of the neurologically dis-organized person.

When we test the neurologically dis-organized person through muscle testing, we find numerous weak muscles. The patterns of weakness vary from individual to individual, but there is an underlying consistency to this pattern.

The following discussion of body systems and reflexes (ie. gait reflexes, cloacal reflexes, stomatognathic systems, cranial systems) is outlined to accomplish two things: (1) to show how the dis-organized body malfunctions, and (2) to show how it affects athletic performance-particularly as it relates to the game of golf. These explanations are not intended to be a complete study of neurologic dis-organization. They are intended to teach basic material about how the body works and how it may be made to function better. We know that normal neurologic integration is a subtle but powerful ally, particularly in athletic performance. The vast majority of golfers and other athletes who have had their bodies restored to normal integration have had positive gains in athletic performance as well as other areas of activity. Their changes have been permanent.

Let's look now at body systems and reflexes of the body that commonly test weak in the neurologically dis-organized person.

Gait Reflexes

Gait testing is done with the individual on an exam table prone or supine. In the supine position the following gait pairs are tested. For extensive study of these tests and the mechanics involved, refer to the bibliography. Our illustration shows the kinesiologist testing the contralateral Shoulder and Hip Flexors, contralateral Shoulder and Hip Extensors, contralateral Shoulder and Hip Abductors, contralateral Shoulder and Hip Adductors, contralateral Psoas Major and Pectoralis Major, and the contralateral Gluteus Medius and Abdominals.

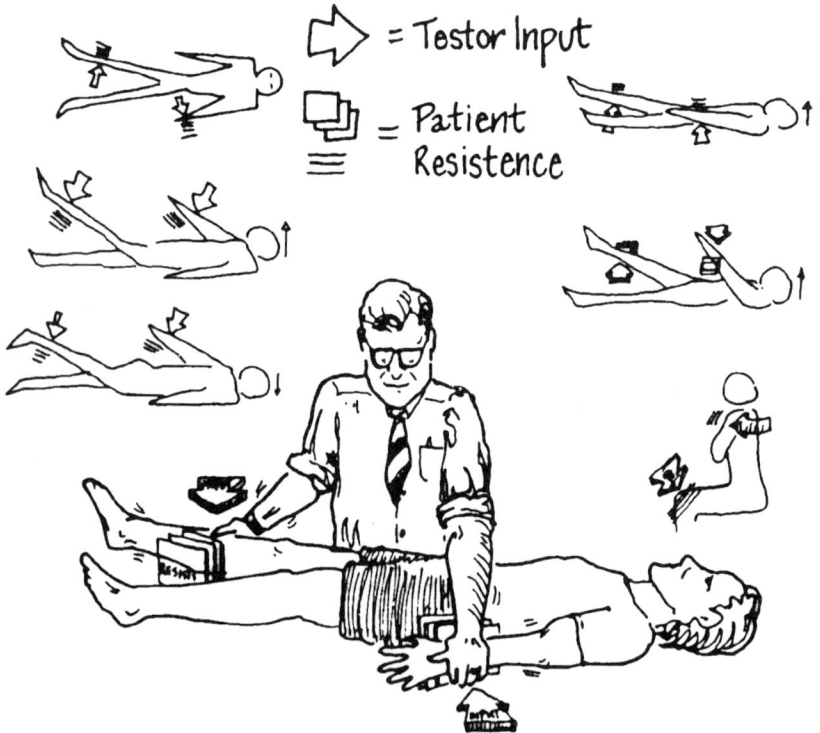

= Testor Input

= Patient Resistence

The overwhelming majority of neurologically dis-organized individuals will test weak on one set of contralateral shoulder and hip flexors as well as contralateral Gluteus Medius and Abdominals. The other gait patterns will also test weak in these people in a random fashion. Individual muscles testing weak in the supine position commonly include the anterior neck flexors, and the abdominal muscles.

Muscles which test "weak" or sub-normal
in the neurologically disorganized individual

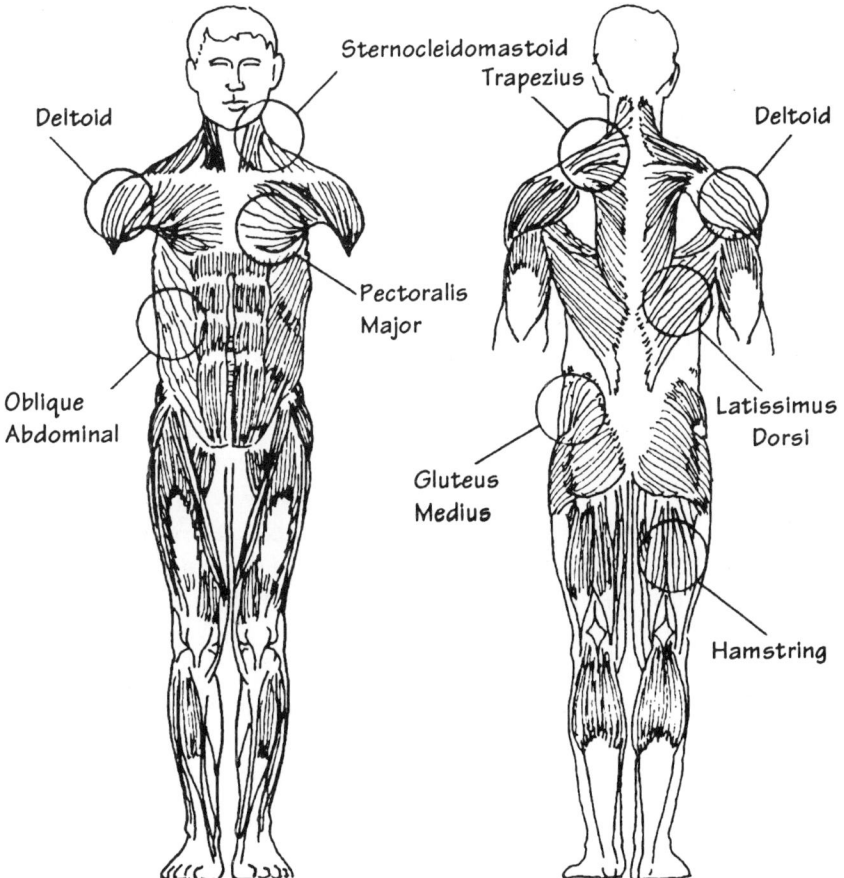

Deltoid

Sternocleidomastoid
Trapezius

Deltoid

Pectoralis
Major

Oblique
Abdominal

Gluteus
Medius

Latissimus
Dorsi

Hamstring

In the upright position (neutral posture) the neurologically dis-organized individual will usually have a weak latissimus dorsi and one or both deltoids will be weak. Stance recovery, when challenged, will be slower than normal. In the stance recovery test, a slight jar to the individual while standing will weaken muscles due to the dis-organization of the body's righting or centering reflexes. There are also muscles from the shoulder girdle to the neck which participate in gait activity in the same way in that some are on (stimulated) while some are off (inhibited) in alternating sequence as one walks or runs. These muscles include the sternocleidomastoid, upper trapezius, deep neck extensors, and the neck flexors. Testing of these muscles individually always shows one or more of them weak in the dis-organized individual.

There is a good deal more to the pattern of neurologic dis-organization than these muscle weaknesses and gait faults. Briefly, the inconsistent communication between brain and body indicated by these weak muscle tests shows that these non-integrated muscle reflexes do not react in normal time, sequence, and power as in the neurologically integrated person. This will affect the timing, rhythm, and power of your golf swing, as well as other aspects of the game.

Cloacal reflexes: head to pelvis synchronization

Muscle testing is used to evaluate the *reflexes of the pelvis* called cloacal reflexes. These are primitive centering reflexes of the pelvis which essentially let the pelvis know where it is in relation to the rest of the body and if it is centered. These reflexes are above the pubic bone in front and bilateral to the tail bone in back. The *labyrinthine reflexes* are located in the middle ear. They are stimulated by movement of the head and they stimulate the postural and neck muscles to help the individual maintain equilibrium head over feet. The *neck righting reflexes* are located at the top of the neck at the skull. They are body position sensors that are important in body orientation and motor coordination.

Body Position Evaluation

The *visual righting reflexes* cause the body to use visual input data to tell the body its orientation in space and whether it is integrated or not. These centering and righting reflexes do exactly that. They help center and right the body by evaluating its position and orientation in space. Then, through communication with the central nervous system they help guide all the muscles which guide the bones which support the body and direct it where you want it and keep it from falling on its face at inopportune moments. Of course, being centered, balanced, and in control of these reflexes is critical in the golf swing.

Proprioception is the body's inner signaling of the position of its parts. The nerves of proprioception are found throughout the body. The proprioceptors are stimulated by the position changes of the body's moving parts. The source of these reflexes is the muscles, tendons and joints, as well as the labyrinth or inner ear mechanism which senses the positions of the head. Altogether, these reflexes sense the balance of the body, awareness of its position and its position in space.

Stomatognathic System (Mouth and Jaw): Connecting the whole body

The stomatognathic system is also important in neurologic organization. The word stomatognathic refers to the mouth and jaw. Dr. David Walther describes the system as the, "complex interaction of structures and function about the head and neck...The system contains components of the bones of the skull, the mandible, the hyoid, the clavicle and the sternum. The muscles and the ligaments; the dento alveolar (tooth) and the temporo mandibular (jaw) joints; the vascular, the lymphatic and the nerve supply systems; the soft tissues of the head; the teeth." Further, "the connection to the sacrum and coccyx by way of the dura mater (envelope around the brain and spinal cord) must be included. A further step includes the innominate bones, completing the pelvis. This system works in an organized manner that depends on normal function of all its parts." (Walther p.344)

To see the stomatognathic system in relation to total body function, realize that this system in conjunction with the pelvis involves the total spinal column. "Structural distortions and dysfunctions throughout the body can disturb pelvic position and motion and spinal function. ...The entire body is included, and ...disturbance in the stomatognathic system can cause health problems almost anywhere in the body, of almost any type..."(Ibid.). That disturbance can also cause neurologic dis-organization. This causes functional disharmony of the body's electromagnetic communication system which forms connecting links of command from brain to body and within the brain itself.

Cranial Bones

The disruption of normal movement of the cranial (skull) bones also has major impact on brain/body integration. The first studies of cranial movement were done in the early 1900's by both osteopaths and chiropractors. These early investigators discovered that there is an independent respiratory movement between the sacrum and the cranium. Investigators learned that the bones of the skull move independently and synchronously with this cranial/sacral respiratory mechanism. Applied Kinesiologists are one of a few groups of specialists in chiropractic, osteopathy, and dentistry who have been effectively using cranial manipulation to treat numerous types of health problems. Disharmony of the movement of cranial bones on their sutures causes disruption in the normal patterns of body function. There are tens of thousands of clinical cases in which individuals received cranial treatment which successfully alleviated body dysfunction (illness). These testify to the importance of proper movement and harmony of the cranial bones and cranial/sacral (head and tail) respiratory mechanism.

Common Causes of Neurologic Disorganization

One may wonder how this marvelous body mechanism gets disrupted in the first place! Trauma to the head is a common cause. Sources of trauma include, first, birth trauma. The stress of movement through the birth canal often is the cause of cranial upset. The babies flexible skull, though, usually corrects itself as the sophisticated cranial/sacral respiratory mechanism is normally self-maintaining and self-correcting.

General head trauma is another cause. Bumps to the head occur in every fashion through childhood and are common in adults as well. Sometimes a hard blow may cause no damage while a light bump has a devastating affect. It depends on individual circumstances.

The hyperflexion/hyperextension injury referred to as "whiplash" is another everyday cause of disorganizing trauma to the system. This type of injury is not just confined to motor vehicle accidents, but is seen frequently in water and snow skiing falls, slip and fall accidents, contact sports and even slamming the wall on the racquetball court. Some forms of dental work with jaw stretching and other stressful procedures in the mouth can be the root cause of disturbed stomatagnathic function.

Clinical factor analyses show the preponderance of individuals that test neurologically dis-organized have been that way since youth. This conclusion is drawn from the proven occurrence in large numbers of children. Adults also report functional affects of dis-organization that they remember from their youth. It is also common to find neurologic dis-organization in infants.

In conclusion, visualize the muscles and ligaments of the body as strands of wire and it's easy to see how the motions of one end of the torso affect the other end and vice-versa. The closed inter-linking of these pieces of the head and pieces of the pelvis through muscles, ligaments, and the spine is called a closed kinematic chain. In the chain when one piece is affected, all pieces are affected. Of course, when one piece is disrupted, all pieces may be disrupted in some way. For these reasons, disturbances of any of the systems discussed above, head, neck, jaw, spine, or pelvis, can cause a chain reaction throughout the musculoskeletal system. Even a gait disruption can upset the active body mechanism. The head bone is indeed connected to the toe bone! From these complex interrelationships one can obviously see that restoration to normal integration can enhance athletic performance.

CHAPTER 9

WHY WE PLAY GOLF
AND COME BACK FOR MORE

PERFORMANCE INTEGRATION^{SM}
THEORY

Performance Integration^{SM} is the application of appropriate stimulus to the human body to enhance and/or restore its ability to integrate its own sensory data with its own behavior. Performance Integration^{SM} addresses wholeness of the brain/body; its purpose is to integrate the performance of the brain/body. The practice and theory of sensory integration are indispensable in the discussion and explanation of Performance Integration^{SM}. The investigators and practitioners of Sensory Integration are to be applauded in their singular accomplishment of bringing reason and logic to bear in a difficult, uncharted field of human neurology and behavior.

"Sensory integration refers to both a neurological process and a theory of the relationship between the neurological process and behavior." (Fisher, Murray, and Bundy, 1991) They further quote Jean Ayres the founder of Sensory Integration theory and practice, who stated;

> "Sensory integration is the neurological process that organizes sensation from one's own body and from the environment, and makes it possible to use the body effectively within the environment. The spatial and temporal aspects of inputs from different sensory modalities are interpreted, associated and unified. Sensory integration is information processing...The brain must select, enhance, inhibit, compare, and associate the sensory information in a flexible, constantly changing pattern: in other words the brain must integrate it."(p.3)

Performance Integration^{SM} and sensory integration theory are remarkably coincident. Sensory integration theory and practice are classically applied to individuals manifesting measurable behavioral and performance disadvantages. Performance Integration^{SM}, though, is a treatment protocol effective on and applied to any individual who demonstrates certain inconsistencies of muscle reaction. This pattern of muscle weakness indicates non-integration and is discovered through Applied Kinesiology. I will reiterate here briefly what was discussed earlier in order to maintain continuity. This non-integration problem for which Performance Integration^{SM} treatment is appropriate occurs in a broad spectrum of people. Most of them do not outwardly demonstrate measurable neurologic disadvantage or "mis-performance". They are not aware of the problem until properly tested with Applied Kinesiology. Indeed, many effects of Performance Integration℠ were not recognized until after numerous clinic patients noted changes in their own behavior following treatment. For example, here is a list of changes experienced by a group of individuals following Performance Integration℠ in a study of 21 aviators and crewmen at Fallon Naval Air Station in 1988. You are probably aware that the aviators of the armed forces are generally in optimum health, mentally alert, and well-trained. They are the "cream of the crop". The men in this study were not aware, prior to their treatment, of any deficiency or disadvantage in their ability or performance. They were thus good candidates to determine whether or not Performance Integration℠ could enhance their performance and/or fitness. While experience is personal and individual their comments suggest that following integration treatment multiple facets of brain activity become better expressed or utilized. They are using the whole brain with more fluidity and consistency. The reports of their experience included:

-Increased ability to deal with cockpit data
-Increased physical and mental awareness in the cockpit
-Less distracted. Quick scan improved and reaction time improved
-G tolerance improved
-Instruments in plane are clearer
-Feel more relaxed when should be
-Improved reaction and thinking
-Better with stress situations, attention span longer
-Sleep better, easier to exercise
-Rest better, more alert
-Energy increased, improved relationship with wife, weight coming off, ball court performance improved
-Improved breath control with swimming, improved rifle shooting, improved knee stability
-Drive easier, less overload
-Sleep better, radio talk improved (aircraft), mid back pain relieved
-Improved peripheral vision
(Porter, Kennedy 1988 Unpublished p.6)

This is evidence that the correction of so called neurologic dis-organization in an individual by Performance Integration^{SM} can and does affect their performance and experience in various ways. "Though difficult to quantify, these subjective reports suggest an enhanced stress tolerance and improved state of well-being. These alone suggest that Performance Integration^{SM} does produce the changes proposed and thus *gives those treated* at the very least *a mental performance/fitness edge.*" (Kennedy and Porter 1989 p.7)

The many changes noted by the aviators as well as the golfers quoted earlier are powerful testimony when viewed with the remarkable changes observed in their muscle tests following integration treatment.

Three aspects of Performance Integration^{SM} theory are key components. First, when your nervous system is normally integrated you pick up sensory information from the environment around you as well as from the position and movement of your body. Your central nervous system then processes and integrates the data collected in order to plan, to organize, and to execute your behavior.

Second, when you are neurologically dis-organized, the planning, organization, and execution of your behavior is compromised in such a way that any one or combination of these operations may be inconsistent or in some way disadvantaged or disabled. Applied Kinesiology testing will demonstrate this lack of integration. This lack of integration further manifests itself as an inconsistency in the expected performance and occurs at any level of human function.

Third, this condition of the body system can be corrected through the treatment protocol called Performance Integration^{SM}. Types of this method of neurologic organization as a specific protocol of treatment have been applied to various maladies of the human organism since at least 1979. The refined approach of Performance Integration^{SM} has been experienced by a few thousand people treated by this author since 1987.

The very nature of the brain/body complex is that it does not lend itself to coldly controlled scientific investigation. Mind processes are subtle, yet very powerful. Applied Kinesiology is a sensitive tool with direct connection to the processes under study. The thousands of people who have experienced the muscle testing procedures of Applied Kinesiology are awed by the phenomena, its discrete power, its repeatability, its value as a tool of diagnosis, and its use as a guide for treatment. Further, the abundance of clinical data and human anecdote continually testify to the wonder of the human organism and its awesome ability when it is integrated and expressing "wholeness".

Thousands of clinical cases reveal, with Applied Kinesiology testing, a repeating pattern of muscle weakness in neurologically dis-organized individuals. When these individuals were treated with Performance Integration^{SM} procedures, the patterns of muscle weakness were reversed. Following correction the vast majority of these individuals experienced positive changes in the performance of their bodies. The broad scope of these changes is apparent in the personal experiences quoted in this book, as well as the research cited. Within these experiences, the changes noted include, but are not limited to:

-Improved hand eye coordination
-Improved perception of visual cues and other sensory information
-Improved body management or use, and balance
-Improved mental utilization and management
-Improved learning ability
-Improved self-confidence, self-esteem, and self-control

The following text will help your understanding of why these changes occurred.

Integration theory makes the following assumptions. First, the brain integrates sensory data in the following circular process.

TOP GOLF

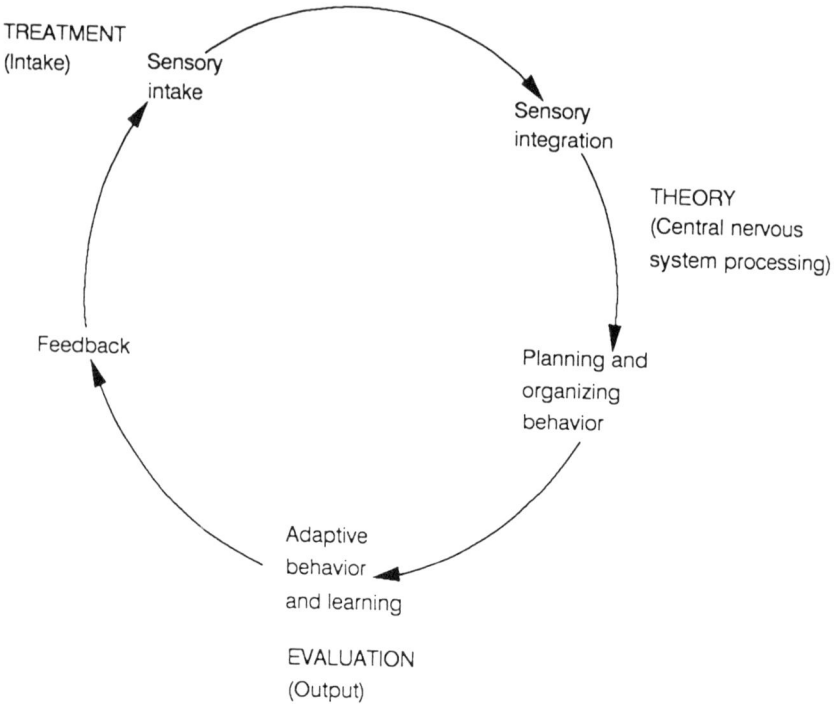

Figure 9.1 The circular process of sensory integration, (Fisher et al,1991, p.5)

You sense it (try it), you integrate it, you change, you feel how it feels, and you do it again.

Second, because it is a circular process, all behavior develops a greater complexity in a step by step repeating process. All behaviors become the foundation of more complex behaviors through integration processes of the brain/body.

Third, the brain function is organized hierarchically. There are higher brain centers involved with reasoning, language, abstraction, and learning. Lower brain centers are concerned with maintenance and survival of the body. The lower levels may influence and control higher levels and vice versa. Obviously the different levels of the brain are constantly interactive, all influencing each other. Important features of the brain and nervous system include the fact that it is an open system that is self-regulating, self-organizing, and self-changing via the circular process. Fourth, your body adapts to change which causes increased complexity of integration which leads to further change, and so on. If you move your body in a new way, for example, learning to swing a golf club, that new movement gives the nervous system new sensation which leads to new integration of the sensation which creates new feelings which feedback to create further adaptation. Again, it is a spiral effect of increased integration and complexity. Further, in the case of movement, the athletic movement of a golf swing, tennis serve, pole vault, or the like, is recorded in the nervous system. The "feel" of it is what guides the athlete's repetition of it. It is "programmed" or "grooved" into the system. Any new sensations or sensed data picked up by hearing, seeing, feeling, smelling, tasting, plus the sensations of body position are organized in the brain. They provide models or memories of how that behavior or action feels. Integration "adapts" these behaviors and provides the foundation for more complex behaviors to be added and integrated. This is why proper practice of a golf swing provides positive growth, while erroneous practice will lock in or adapt poor performance. For this reason, it is hard to break old habits. Also, this means that if we perform better in any way, we have successfully adapted a new behavior.

Fifth, it appears that we have an innate drive to develop this "integration" of the senses. We do things that challenge us to adapt more complex behaviors. In other words, we have a motivation to grow. This is a basic survival instinct to create circumstances that feel good to us. This must include mental, physical and emotional challenges, whether they be closing real estate deals or bettering our last golf game.

Look at Figure 9.2 below. Moving left to right we progress using the basic senses through their integration to the end products of mastering behavior. We perceive, confront, explore, manipulate, and then execute a behavior. Moving left to right, also, the survival senses with which we are all programmed begin to accumulate data. As the data is loaded in our computers, it is "interpreted, associated and unified". Note that we all begin on the left of the table with very primitive action. Moving to the right, as we mature, collect more data, and integrate the data, we move toward self-actualization at much higher levels. Keep in mind that actualize means to "make real" or to "realize", and self-actualization is "to realize fully one's potential". The right side of the chart represents successful adaptation as a general end product of neurologic integration, or integration of the senses. Interestingly, the higher levels of integration are represented by our volitional expression accompanied by our attendant self-perceptions. We think, act, feel, and generally perform at higher levels.

THE SENSES → **INTEGRATION OF THEIR INPUTS** → **END PRODUCTS**

THE SENSES	INTEGRATION OF THEIR INPUTS	END PRODUCTS	
Auditory (hearing)	speech, language	ability to concentrate	S
			E
Vestibular (gravity) and movement — eye movements, posture		ability to organize	L
			F
balance, muscle tone	body percept, coordination of two sides of the body	self-esteem	A
			C
gravitational security	motor planning	self-control	T
	eye-hand coordination		U
Proprioceptive (muscles and joints)	activity level	self-confidence	A
	visual perception		L
sucking	attention span, activity	academic learning ability	I
	purposeful		Z
eating	emotional stability	capacity for abstract	A
		thought and reasoning	T
Tactile (touch) — mother-infant bond, tactile comfort			I
		specialization of each side of	O
Visual (seeing)		the body and the brain	N

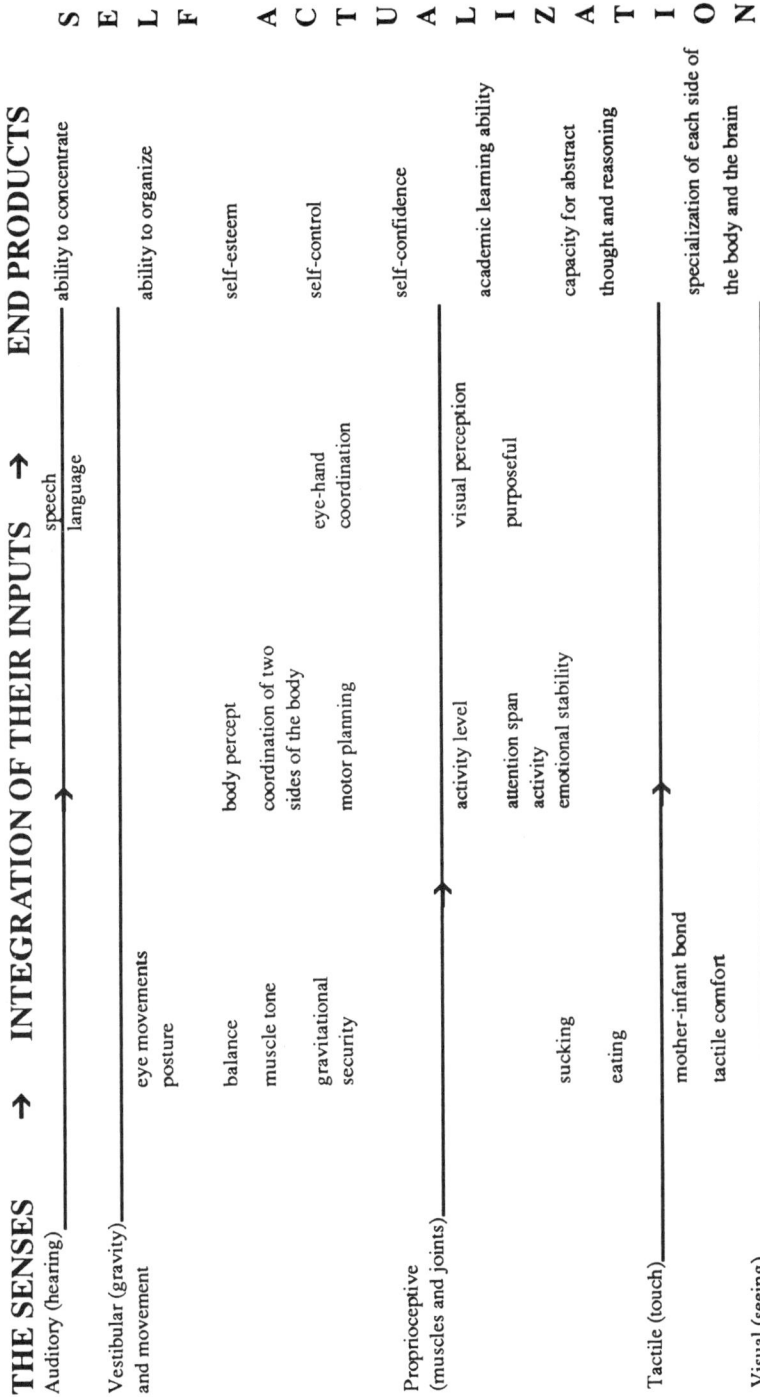

Figure 9.2   The Senses, Integration of Their Inputs, and Their End Products (Ayres 1979)

SENSES → **INTEGRATION OF SENSATIONS** → **END PRODUCTS OF INTEGRATION**

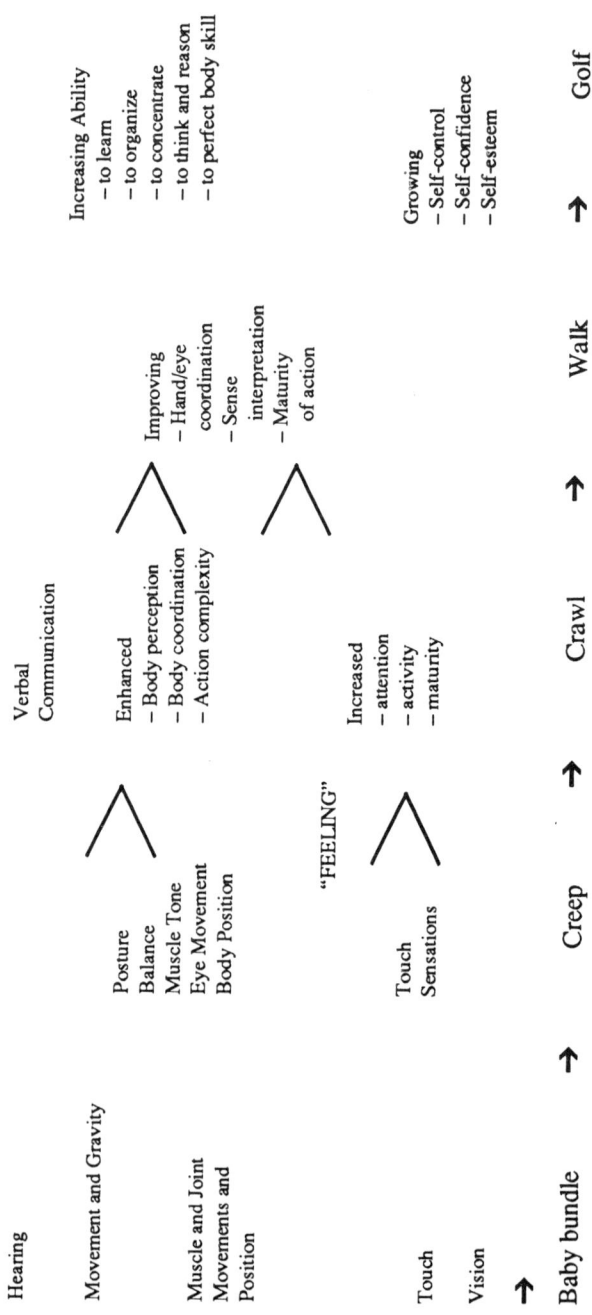

Hearing

Movement and Gravity

Muscle and Joint Movements and Position

"FEELING"

Touch

Vision

↑

Verbal Communication

Posture
Balance
Muscle Tone
Eye Movement
Body Position

Enhanced
– Body perception
– Body coordination
– Action complexity

Touch Sensations

Increased
– attention
– activity
– maturity

Improving
– Hand/eye coordination
– Sense interpretation
– Maturity of action

Increasing Ability
– to learn
– to organize
– to concentrate
– to think and reason
– to perfect body skill

Growing
– Self-control
– Self-confidence
– Self-esteem

Baby bundle → Creep → Crawl → Walk → Golf

Figure 9.3   Integration of the Golfer

THE COMPLETE GOLF SWING EXPERIENCE
Integration of their input

The Senses	Mental Assessment of Situation	Organization and Preparation	Execution	End Results
Auditory Hearing Inner self talk and analysis Set up check lists	*Goal Assessment* – desirability – attainability	Brain/body Readiness Analysis Action Planning > Command	*Semi-automatic* Take away	*INCREASED* – ability to concentrate – ability to organize – learning ability
Vestibular Gravity and Movement Body relative to the ground	*Resource Assessment* Body Position – posture – tension – stance – etc.	*Body placement over ball* – position – posture – stance – tension	*Changing body position* Arm Hand Leg Pelvis Shoulder Neck Head Spine	– capacity for reasoning – specialization of brain and body – self confidence
Proprioceptor Muscles and joints Body relative to itself Head, hands, feet positions	*Body* – agility – flexibility	– weight distribution – club set feel	*ACTION COORDINATION* Takeaway Turn Wrist cock Leg bend Foot lift Up shift Top swing Down swing Body turn Follow through	– self-control – self-esteem
Tactile Touch Feel/outside		– grip tension – grip strength – weight distribution or feel – body to body contact – clothes comfort		
Visual Vision	*Situation Assessment* – lie of ball – club selection – pin position – yardage – hazards – etc.	– club alignment – ball position – target position – body alignment		– motivation to repeat

Figure 9.4   The golf swing as the brain/body sees it, start to finish.

Clinically, a commonly felt change following the Performance Integration℠ treatment is an experience or manifestation of greater self-confidence in the individual. Reviewing the roles of the integrated brain/body regarding self-perception and mental function in Figures 9.2, 9.3, and 9.4 we see why. The integrated person has improved utilization of both brain hemispheres and greater facility with complex functions of the brain. This can't help but provide a new *sense* of self and thus, greater self-confidence. To demonstrate what we are seeking in the golf experience it is interesting to read what our integrated golfers say about self-confidence. They are saying that integration has led them toward the self-realization end of the integration products table.

"I feel like I am balanced. I don't panic over shots. I don't worry about the drive. And if it's true line fairway or if it's a wedge over a bunker to a tight pin position, then maybe I shouldn't be shooting at it. But the thing is, I am confident enough to give it a try, and if it fails, a negative portion of that shot doesn't bother me. It's one of those things that I feel at home in that environment. I feel I can get it up and down, even if I miss what I am looking for. It's just increased confidence."
P.L. male professional

"It's a situation now where there's a lot of intuitiveness involved in my club selection. I may not even want the yardage. I may want to stand over it because I know the club is going to hit it there. It's a much greater feeling of confidence now, knowing that. I will say that I have increased the length of hit with every club in my bag."
G.R. male professional

"I feel inside myself more confidence. I don't walk out there and say "Hey, I'm going to birdie this hole." I just seem to get up there with much more confidence in my structure and my stance, everything seems to be much more coordinated. Performance Integration℠ is the only thing I have done."
N.L. male amateur

The innate drive to feel the positive effects of new adaptive behaviors created as a product of integrated senses leads the integrated person to try new experiences and meet new challenges. This is a drive to self-mastery and it is self-perpetuating. In turn, success achieved leads to further motivation to master other aspects of life. Following integration, people tend to have more enthusiasm and confidence. They then seek activities which provide greater self-actualization or growth promoting experience. These, in turn, through the spiral process of self-actualization, provide feedback which further enhances senses and integration. This is called flow. "Flowing, a flow experience, the organization of the self is more complex than it had been before. It is by becoming increasingly complex that the self might be said to grow". (Csikzentmihalyi, 1990 p.41) Study of the spirals of self-actualization will help you "integrate" the theory of Performance Integration^{SM}.

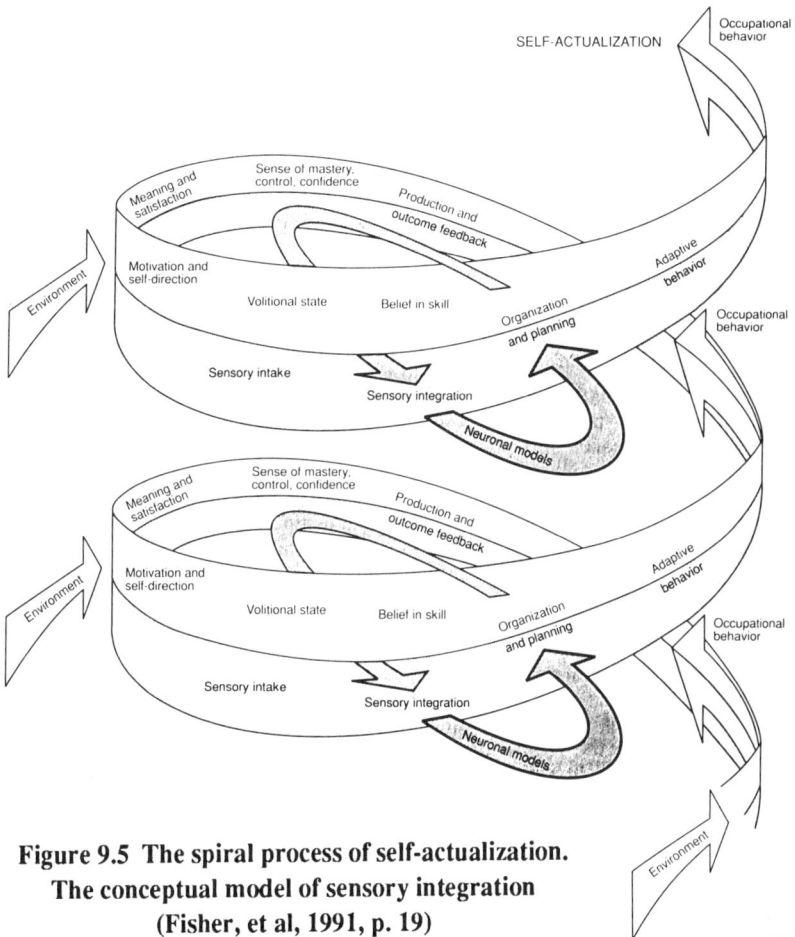

Figure 9.5 The spiral process of self-actualization.
The conceptual model of sensory integration
(Fisher, et al, 1991, p. 19)

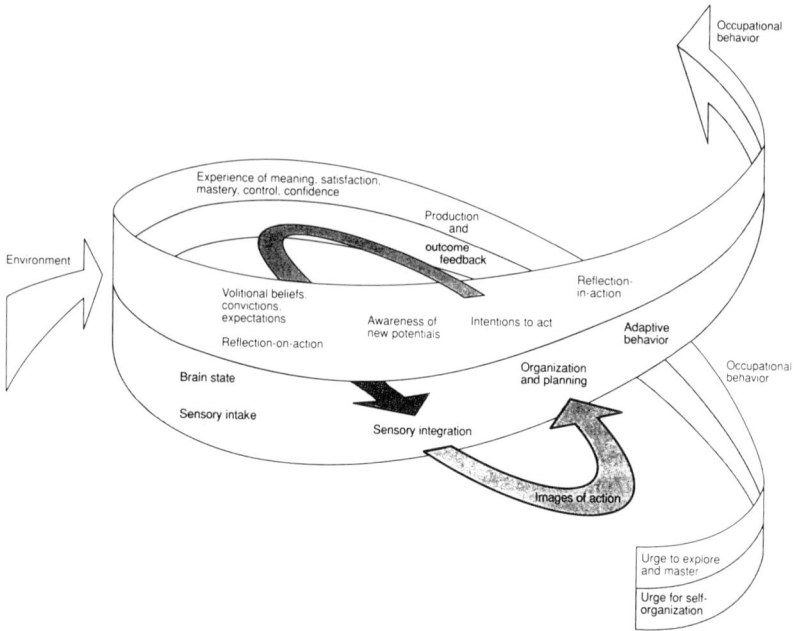

Occupational
behavior

Experience of meaning, satisfaction,
mastery, control, confidence

Production
and
outcome
feedback

Environment

Reflection-
in-action

Volitional beliefs,
convictions,
expectations
Reflection-on-action

Awareness of
new potentials

Intentions to act

Adaptive
behavior

Brain state

Organization
and planning

Occupational
behavior

Sensory intake

Sensory integration

Images of action

Urge to explore
and master

Urge for self-
organization

**Figure 9.6 Synchronous interdependence of mind and brain-body
superimposed on the sequential spiral process of self-actualization.
(Fisher, et al, 1991, p. 36)**

Because we are speaking to the phenomena of neurologic dis-organization, we should note how the self-actualization process breaks down if dis-organization is present. For sensory integration to occur "the central nervous system must actively process, organize, and modulate sensory inputs from the body and the environment. A normal sensory integrative process implies an organized and appropriate response to sensory intake" (Fisher, 1991 p.20). In the neurologically dis-organized subject these processes may or may not occur or may occur inconsistently.

Common statements of post-organization treatment individuals include that they are more confident, coordinated, centered, and motivated. These individuals report their experience with many self-actualization words. They talk about being more "centered" or "together", having things go more smoothly in their lives, or not getting as "stressed out" as they did prior to treatment. The root of this self-actualization process is indicated by the upper spiral of the previous illustrations. Humans by nature pursue various occupations, work, play, learning, and self-maintenance because of intrinsic motivation. Action in these activities is motivated by the desire for mastery and achievement. The action experience introduces new data into the brain/body. The program for a skill, then, not only includes the sensory and motor components of the skill (the bottom spiral), but the sense of confidence, self-mastery and control that provide meaning and satisfaction once the skill is mastered (shown by the top spiral). We may deduce that if individuals experience enhanced self-perceptions and self-mastery along with enhanced skill following Performance Integration℠, then neurologic dis-integration was inhibiting their development of these important character and physical traits. Dis-integration retards or disrupts movement up the self-actualization spiral. It is more difficult for the non-integrated individual to master a skill or improve than it is for the integrated individual.

The reader can appreciate the difficulty in measuring changes of this type which are admittedly subjective. The incidence and repetition of these experiences, though, shows that correction of neurologic dis-organization does powerfully impact the performance of the individual in many facets of life. You recall our discussion of the aviators who were tested by computer after integration treatment. The computer measurements showed that they had enhanced eye/hand coordination, better short term memory, and improved sense of perceptual rotation (body in space). These results suggest that some neurologic integration changes can be measured with proper control.

In our life's activities what we as individuals are doing is reacting to, or acting on, the environment to develop or enhance some control of it. *Inner Game of Golf* (1981) author Gallwey said, "Away from the golf course, I took a fresh look at the game and asked myself what it was all about. The single word that came to mind was control. Basically, it seemed to be a matter of getting your body to do what you want it to do so that you can make the golf ball do what you want it to do. I saw the game as a stark challenge to a person's ability to control his own body" (p.4).

People are actively trying to master new skills of survival or function at new levels, perhaps learning to read, to drive a car, to swing a golf club, or to sell an insurance policy. There are some important qualifications in these pursuits. They include whether the activity is meaningful (does it have value or purpose), does the person understand it, and do they feel in control? If it does have meaning, the stimulus is to move forward and learning is automatic. If meaning is not perceived, as in the disinterested student trying to learn physics, or a reluctant spouse learning to play golf, then learning falters. The level of meaning does govern the level of mastery of the new behavior. No interest (no meaning) leads to no mastery. Lack of understanding can also stifle movement up the spiral towards mastery. One might simply not communicate at the level of either a teacher or system under study. Lack of control might be as rudimentary as trying to play golf with left handed clubs when you are right handed. Together or individually, meaning, understanding and control stimulate and enable movement up the spiral of self-actualization.

To acquire a new skill it is touched, seen, smelled, heard, tasted and experienced by the brain/body. It travels through loops of production and outcome feedback. The central nervous system then adapts behavior through its processing, organizing, and modulation of the sensory data. The brain/body then creates neural models or maps to master and recreate and enhance the new skill. The reader can see why the spiral is necessary to explain the model of self-actualization. The acquisition of a new skill forms the foundation of further adaptive behavior and mastery of greater skill in this endless ascending spiral.

Now, more exciting is to understand what this has to do with "self-actualization". Humans have an innate drive to "do something". They want to pursue meaningful pursuits whether it be work, play, leisure, or self-maintenance. Mastery of any of these occupations through the adaptive behaviors created through sensory integration leads to feedback of meaning and satisfaction in achievement. In reference again to Gallwey's postulate that golf is about control, Czikszenmihalyi states, "Getting in control of life is never easy, and sometimes it can be definitely painful. But in the long run optimal experiences add up to a sense of mastery or perhaps better, a sense of *participation* in determining the content of life, that comes as close to what is usually meant by happiness as anything else we can conceivably imagine"(p.4). Mastering golf can be about participation in determining the content of life. A study of adults "at play" was reported by Czikszenmihalyi in 1979. The study surveyed occupations ranging from chess and basketball to rock climbing, surgery, and secretarial work. The results throughout the occupations revealed these experiences in the individuals participating: they reported that when they were at a peak of involvement in their occupation they experienced clear, focused, undisturbed concentration, as well as a clear, non-contradictory goal. They received immediate feedback such as where the ball went when hit or whether they finished the task. Also there was a sense of time compression or timelessness as if time passed too quickly or unnoticed. These people felt a control of affect or influence and with that control a kind of "loss of ego". Still the sense of self was stronger following the activity. Further, their involvement was so deep and intense that they lost awareness of the concerns of everyday life. The characteristics of this state included meeting a challenge that resulted in development of a greater sense of self-confidence, self-control, and self-mastery. Czikszenmihalyi says, "Now these are all the subjective characteristics of the state of involvement or experience which we call the flow state because it's a native term that many people, such as composers of music, rock climbers, etc, spontaneously produce in talking about this. It's like flowing, it's like being carried away and yet being in control of the direction of the flow"(p.261) He further discusses "flow" as occurring when an individual meets the "just right challenge", or that challenge which is matched to the individual's ability. When a challenge is greater than the individual's ability, it tends to produce anxiety and worry. The challenge that is less than the individual's ability leads to boredom. The challenge of activity at a person's relative skill level is what produces the state of "Flow" and all its accompanying positive feelings and emotions. What we are after is that state and it's attendant feelings. We seek the flow state even for brief moments, but the state itself can be maintained for long periods, including 18 holes of golf.

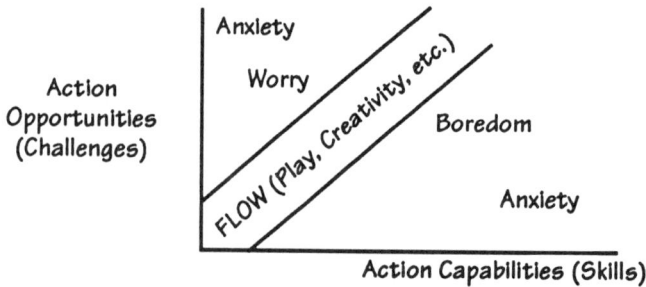

Model of the Flow State. When action opportunities are perceived by the actor to overwhelm his capabilities, the resulting stress is experienced as anxiety. When the ratio of capabilities is higher, the experience is worry. The state of flow is felt when opportunities for action are in balance with the actor's skills. The experience is then autotelic. When skills are greater than opportunities for using them, the state of boredom results, which again fades into anxiety when the ratio becomes too large.

(Adapted from Csikszentmihayli, 1975 a)

Let's take another look at what we've described as integration and how it leads to flow. At birth, your body system is instinctive about things like hunger and discomfort while it has little, if any, volitional control over body movement. You can't reach and hold, grasp with your hands, crawl, roll over, etc. (In contrast to humans, a newborn lamb is on its feet within minutes of birth—a programmed instinct prompted by its mother.) The brain/computer software is programmed by your senses—what you see, feel, taste, touch, and hear. This information travels via the nerves to the brain/computer which files, collates, interprets, and organizes the data. This is sensory integration.

Watch a child discover his hand or foot. "Touch," "Feel," and "See" data pours into the computer and the computer processes it. Soon the child learns about his feet and hands and where they are in relation to each other. He starts grasping things and discovering other uses for his hands and so on. As time passes, the child progresses from creeping to crawling and then to walking. The brain, meanwhile, is collecting data from the external and internal senses. These internal senses include such data collection as head position, joint nerve reflexes and muscle positions (proprioception). These tell the brain where the body parts are and how they are relating to each other. This data is added to the external senses of sight, touch, hearing, smell, and taste. The data from the senses integrates in the computer to tell the head its relationship to the feet, how the weight shifts on the feet, and everything else about where body parts are and their activity. This occurs with ever increasing complexity as we develop. Activities are pursued for the sake of self-maintenance, work, play, and leisure to satisfy that intrinsic drive for mastery and meaning. The child will wiggle, creep, crawl, walk, run, dance, play golf, and so on. Each event is increasing in complexity and moving up the self-actualization spiral.

One might have a spiral of self-actualization rising from arithmetic through math to trigonometry, calculus, quantum physics, and more. This process involves ever increasing complexity, ever increasing mastery, and ever increasing self-actualization. There can be spirals for cooking, landscaping, mechanical engineering, playing basketball, playing golf, parenting, language, and so on ad infinitum. The spirals are independent, interdependent, and codependent. Looking again at the spiral we see that everything we do, every act we perform in life, must go through this process. The simple acts of daily self-maintenance, academic learning, and other skill acquisition require the same development process. We all program our own "computer" or brain/body this way.

Imagine, if you will, the variety of self-actualization spirals we each have. It includes your "golf" spiral. At the bottom of the spiral is that first handling of the club, its feel and heft, and how it stretches the shoulder in a clean sweeping swing. You think at the same time you could knock somebody silly with the thing. That's part of the spiral, that thought and all those feelings. You also feel the teeth rattling thud of the clubhead digging a trench before the ball and hear your instructor saying, "you started the swing with your hands instead of your hips". These are bits of data incorporated in the spiral, even those feelings and inputs you care never to feel or hear again. Then the embarrassment of practice hoping no one will suspect you are a novice. After all, your spiral is loaded with the opinions (imagined or real) of possibly the whole world regarding you and your golf abilities. It twists upward and outward in an expanding nature away from those struggling early days of your golf experience. Yet the early spiral is there, easily retrieved by some deja-vu event that stimulates an engram (simultaneous meaningful events) that lets you know you've been there. Then, on that road to self-actualization are two or three- and then dozens and even hundreds of near perfect golf shots and their attendant body physiology and psychology. Perhaps you created self-stimulating cues in order to duplicate the good shots. Early on those good shots are casual and coincidental. As time passes, they become more frequent by design, as you incorporate formal and informal instruction. You also read a lot about golf and begin to relate more closely with the golfer's experience as your own spiral of the golf experience expands further. Also on the spiral are many games with friends old and new. These are games in all sorts of weather conditions, all times of day. There are successes and failures from simple shots to total tournaments. You may have branched or mini-spirals for each club in your bag, for each hole on your local course, and so on. These spirals contribute to the overall achievement of your full potential in golf. You begin to master each one of the tools of golf and circumstances of their use in pursuit of mastery. This is adaptation. This is brain organization. They are innate.

This same golf experience has many other elements involved. For instance, your consideration of those things which compete with your "self-actualization" trek in the world of golf. They may include your spouse's feelings about your pursuit, the things you've left behind, the sacrifices, the expense, the worth, and so on. All together they represent increasing complexity, adaptation and mastery.

Now go back once more to look at the list of end products of integration, and compare them with the end products of your self-actualization spiral for golf. As you have progressed building your spiral of golf haven't you increased your ability to concentrate, ability to organize, self-esteem, self-control, self-confidence, learning ability, and capacity for thought and reasoning?

"Adaptiveness implies mastery over the environment rather than mastery of the person by the environment. When the individual feels in control of the environment, the locus of control is internal, within the individual, rather than external. The person who develops this sense of mastery also develops a belief in his or her own abilities; that is, belief in skill. The realization of having the ability to do something enables one to become self-directing, and the individual becomes motivated to explore his or her capacity through the planning and production of adaptive behaviors, and the participation in meaningful occupation" (Fisher, 1991, p.22). Thus, we have an innate drive to self-actualization through mastery of a meaningful skill. Golf!

Further study of Figure 9.2, 9.3, and 9.4 will provide an appreciation not only of the progressive affects of normal integration, but also some of the critical end products. One doesn't ordinarily think of the ability to concentrate, the ability to organize, and self-confidence as being the result of normal development, but they are. For the best performance of an individual to occur, their natural integration must progress normally and remain whole. Consider simply how important it is to any focused activity to have the subtle, yet powerful allies of self-control, reasoning ability, and clear ability to organize thought and to produce action. In athletics, the applications are obvious and overwhelming. Athletic events or efforts represent a pinnacle expression of a life activity. One of the major appeals of athletic competition is that it brings to focus these "end products" of human integration. It expresses the best of an individual at his best. What normal individual wouldn't desire these "end products" of normal integration and their attendant feelings?

Notice the similarity between the reported experiences/feeling/emotions of the individuals in the state of "Flow" and the end products indicated for sensory integration. Further, note the clinical reports of the individuals who received Performance Integration^{SM} treatment. They are strikingly coincident, and they support the theory that a normally functioning, integrated nervous system is much more able to achieve and maintain flow states, or stay "in the zone" as they say. What we now know is that the state of "Flow" may elude us due to a normal stress reflex that gets stuck in the brain/body. This is called neurologic dis-organization. A highly developed and refined technology is available to discover this problem and to correct it. This technology, Performance Integration^{SM} can remarkably affect the golfer's ability to consistently play "in the zone".

CHAPTER 10

PERFORMANCE INTEGRATION[SM] TREATMENT

A REMARKABLE PHENOMENON

The development and refinement of the Performance Integration^{SM} protocol is remarkable in itself. Constant effort to discover that procedure which would consistently produce desired results has led to the treatment briefly outlined here. First, muscles are tested to determine if the subject has the pattern of muscle response that indicates neurologic dis-organization. Next, if the tests are positive, reflex adjustments are given. Each specific muscle test that is weak is used to discover the subject's counteractive body reflex point. That reflex is stimulated and the muscle weakness disappears. The reflex stimulus is a light tap.

The subject lies supine on a treatment table as the doctor repeatedly tests muscles and stimulates counteractive reflexes. The treatment is generally painless and takes only a few minutes. The apparent simplicity of it is quite remarkable as years of clinical research were required to achieve this highly refined Performance Integration^{SM}.

To perform the treatment, the doctor follows a specific pattern of progress in testing and treatment. It is this protocol that is the key to complete and permanent resolution of the dis-organization. The eight treatments necessary to correct the condition are administered in a 2 to 4 day period.

Results of great variety, subtle to profound, may appear anywhere from one to one hundred days after treatment. The brain/body willingly adapts to this integration. Changes are readily obvious to the golfer who plays frequently and has a real sense of his body. Some cases do not perceive change without thorough self-inspection and self-analysis. In all cases after treatment muscle tests of the originally weak muscles remain strong and symmetric.

A few golfers have reported positive results in areas not directly connected to their golf game. The majority, though, have found early on very meaningful and significant change in their golf performance. As the golf game is sensitive to what generally is going on with the player in all facets of life, we can safely say that any positive change in any of that life will reflect positively on the golf course.

Interestingly, no negative affects have ever been reported by any treated individuals. There have been a few complaints of having to adjust to yardage gains in the long game, but adaptation has been readily and happily made. Most golfers after Performance Integration^{SM} have to explain their somewhat remarkable improvements to skeptical and surprised playing companions. Repetition of the treatment is not necessary when properly done. Once is enough, and results last indefinitely. In only a handful of instances has repeated treatment been necessary. In each case the subjects had experienced significant subsequent head trauma.

CHAPTER 11

GOLF IS LIFE
LIFE IS GOLF

Top Golfers speak of changes in their lives that are beyond golf. Golf is life is golf?!

From a concentration or focus standpoint, I think that's—again in my own mind—it's related to that patience. If I am more patient, and I don't get that aggressive streak in me, my concentration and focus is tremendously better than it normally is, you know, in my golf game and in my work and in my own personal life with the kids. M.M.

I think my energy level is a little higher right now simply because after the first, I think, three treatments, I noticed a big difference in my sleeping habits. I seemed to be getting maybe not quite as much sleep, but the sleep I was getting was better sleep.

The focus part seems to be pretty easy. I just—normally, when I work in the summertime, I worked anywhere from 12 to 14 hours teaching, and it would be very difficult giving the last four or five lessons because the day was so long. Now, it doesn't seem to be as strenuous, as difficult. B.S.

I felt not as moody, and I felt more energy, and I slept better. I just had a positive reaction. I felt real good about my life, about things, about my body. Everything kind of was— kind of went together.

Well, you know, pretty much before integration, I was more uptight. I don't know, I wasn't as relaxed. I just feel very content. And I think more than anything, it has helped that way. L.E.

The subtleness, it would have to be my feelings inside, just more peace of mind, more contentedness, happier without even realizing that I was—all of a sudden it hit me, that hey, life is better. I feel better. I feel like I am living now instead of just worrying and trying to conquer my problems. R.H.

Well, the biggest change is now I know where my feet are. I was the klutz of the world. I trip. I would—I have been tripping through life for over 45 years. I just— I was amazed that I know where my feet are now. I have not tripped, have not fallen or bumped into something since my integration. And I have a lot of energy, too. I feel really energized. P.W.

The wonderful thing, on a day-to-day basis, is the lack of stress and the total concept of feeling in charge of your body. I don't know how to really, really stress that I am in charge now. I feel good. I feel energetic. I am aware of things. I am on top of things, and that's a power feeling. You're not controlled by any needs to do something. You are in charge, and if something requires your reference, you're there 100 percent energetically, mentally and physically. You are charged. And boy, I just love this feeling. I can't wait to live from day to day. I love each day's different experience because I am in charge. I am living. It— it's not happening. I am living. J.W.

Well, some things changed in my life. And the only thing I have done in the last few months different in my routine has been integration. So, I would say it has made a real big difference in allowing me to tap into the inner part of me is that gentle, kind relaxed part that sometimes our daily routines don't allow us to find. So, a big difference. J.U.

After about the fourth visit, and it's hard to explain; but I felt something mentally with me. I mean, I am not a morning person, I have never been; but now I find myself waking up before the alarm gets up and go and get to work. I find myself much more focused at work. The concentration is unbelievable. R.C.

It is amazing to me, and I noticed it right away, the mellow-ness. I am able to handle tense situations a lot better now than I have in the past, better able to deal with them in the business that I am in now.

With my clients, I think that I tend to be less quick now, and I listen better. I have found, since this thing, that I listen better; I think because of that, I have been able to give my clients better advice because I listen to what they say probably better than I have before.

My life, I'm just more in control, and I think that's the same thing about my golf game. I mean both of them are more in control. J.M.

I really believe that I have a much lower stress level; and I really could handle more things without getting uptight about it. I would have some of my sales people that would come in that were uptight, and I was able to just stay calm, so they walked out calm. I really do attribute that to the program. B.M.

I am able to cope with stressful moments a little better now. I think before, I used to react quicker than I do now. Now, I take little more time in reacting to the situation. N.D.

After the integration, I can make decisions and feel comfortable with them. I felt comfortable with myself and able to continue my work and know that I was doing a good job, and I gave my best. I wasn't tired, and I could keep going. Where before, I would burn out and be gone. S.W.

I don't get as tired as I used to get. I have more energy, less stress. I have never been someone that has a very— I have a very low stress problem to begin with, but I noticed that I enjoy getting up and going to work more. I enjoy going out because I knew I was going to be able to really help people. G.R.

That's probably one of the biggest changes I have experienced. I am a lot more casual in my performance as far as an instructor. My day-to-day relationships with my family and with those that I am close to, it seems to be a lot less stressful. I feel I am just kind of going with the flow as life hands me those types of things. B.H.

Personally, I have never felt such confidence. I have been more creative in the last two months than I have been in the last five years. I can sit down and write things that would take me, you know, hours to think about. Now, I just write it down, and it turns out great. It's wonderful. A.D.

BIBLIOGRAPHY

Ayres, A.J., *Sensory Integration and Learning Disorders*, Western Psychological Services Los Angeles, 1972-3.

Cochran, A. and Stobbs, J., *The Search for the Perfect Swing*, The Golf Society of Great Britain, Whitehall Court, London S.W.1., 1986

Creutzfeldt, O., Schmidt, R., Willis, W., Ed, Impasses and Fallacies of the Brain-Mind Discussion, *Sensory-Motor Integration in the Nervous System*, SpringerVerlag, New York,(32-41), 1984.

Csikszentmihalyi, M., *Flow*, New York, Harper Collins, 1990.

Csikszentmihalyi, M., Sutton-Smith, B., editor, The Concept of Flow, *Play and Learning*, Gardner Press, New York, 1979.

Dennison, Paul E., *Switching On*, Edukinesthetics, Inc., Glendale, CA., 1981

Fisher, A., Murray, E., Bundy, A. Ed., *Sensory Integration: theory and practice*. F.A. Davis Co, Philadelphia, 1991.

Gallwey, T., *The Inner Game of Golf*, Random House, New York., 1981.

Graham, David, *Your Way to Winning Golf*, Golf Digest/Tennis, Inc., 1985.

Hebron, M. *See and Feel the Inside Move The Outside*, self published., 1984.

Hogan, Ben, *Five Lessons- The Modern Fundamentals of Golf*, Simon and Schuster, Inc, New York, 1957.

Jobe, F., and Schwab, D., *30 Exercises for Better Golf*, Champion Press, Inglewood, CA., 1986.

Jobe, F. Perry, J., Pink, M., Electromyographic shoulder activity in men and women professional golfers, *The American Journal of Sports Medicine*, v.17, no.6,782-787, 1989.

Kelly, Homer, *The Golfing Machine*, Star System Press, Seattle, 1982.

Kennedy, R and Porter, C., *F. Petho Technical Memorandum*, Institute of Human Achievement Technology, 26 January 1989.

Kubistant, Tom, *Performing Your Best*, Life Enhancement Publications, Champaign, Illinois,1986.

Leadbetter, David, *The Golf Swing*, Viking Penguin, New York, 1990.

Murphy, Michael, *Golf in the Kingdom*, Viking Penguin, New York, 1992.

Palmer, A., *My Game and Yours*, Simon and Schuster, Inc., New York., 1983

Perry, Jaquelin, *Gait Analysis- Normal and Pathological Function*, Slack, Inc., New Jersey, 1992.

Pink, M., Jobe, F., Perry, J., Electromyographic Analysis of the shoulder during the golf swing, *The American Journal of Sports Medicine*, v.18 no.2,137-40., 1990.

Pribram, K. , The Cognitive Revolution and Mind Brain Issues, *American Psychologist*, v.41, no.5, 507-520, 1986.

Walther, D.S., *Applied Kinesiology, Volume I- Basic Procedures and Muscle Testing*, Systems D.C., Pueblo, Co., 1981.

Walther, D.S., *Applied Kinesiology, Volume II- Head, Neck and Jaw Pain and Dysfunction,- the Stomatognathic System*, Systems D.C., Pueblo, Co., 1983.

Walther, D.S., *Applied Kinesiology- Synopsis*, Systems D.C., Pueblo, Co., 1988.

Wiren, Gary and Coop, Richard, *The New Golf Mind*, Simon and Schuster, New York, 1978.

APPENDIX

TOP GOLFER
INTERVIEW TRANSCRIPTS

M.M. male golf professional

Q. You've recently experienced the treatment called Performance Integration. What is your initial reaction?

A. I had planned to play a lot more golf than I have played but what I have found is I have been a lot more competitive than I would have been without practicing and going out and hitting a few balls every day. I have found since I've been integrated I can go out and play once or twice a month and be very competitive. I have won a couple Pro/Ams and been in the top few spots in the others, and I am a lot more relaxed and comfortable. I just seem to be a notch up or a little more sharp than I had been in the past when I don't play.

Q. So, you seem to retain your ability from game to game?

A. Yeah, in the past it has been like I had to learn it over or go out and spend a couple days practicing. Right now, I feel like I can go out and play and stay sharp from game to game without a lot of practice in between. And when you're as busy as I am, that's a big bonus.

Q. What are the specific factors of your game that you have seen a change in?

A. One of the primary things that I have noticed is that I am a lot more patient than I used to be on the golf course. When I didn't put a lot of time in my golf game, I would play and wait for something bad to happen. Now, I can go out and I am a lot more relaxed and patient, and I feel like I can sustain the good play through the round. And it's just a more pleasurable experience because I am keeping the wheels on.

Q. Would you say there are any changes in your long game, specifically?

A. I have always been a pretty good driver of the golf ball. I am a little bit more consistent as far as direction off the tee. I am keeping it in play a little better. I think a lot of it is I have a tendency to get swinging pretty hard at it, and I have been able to maintain my tempo from start to finish a lot better than I had in the past. And that falls under the patience category. I am just more patient out there than I usually have been in the past. I don't play a lot of golf. My golf swing tends to get very quick, and I have been able to go out and keep the tempo, and as a result, my long game, especially driving the golf ball, has been a lot better.

Q. Are you in more regulation?

A. I hit more greens in regulation. In fact, the last round I played, I hit 17 greens in regulation.

Q. Say something about your control.

A. The control comes, for me, in keeping in tempo. If I keep my golf swing in tempo, and I hit it straight and I hit it long, the tempo thing and the patience thing are kind of related for me. If I stay patient and don't get edgy on the golf course and want to hit it, be more aggressive, my control is a lot better. And because I have maintained better patience and tempo during a round I am hitting a lot more fairways and a lot more greens.

Q. What about your game management?

A. Again, I am just a lot more relaxed out there. I start out with the first couple holes missing birdie putts, and I don't get worried about it because I think I'm going to hit more good shots. And from that standpoint I can sustain the good play all the way through a round. In the past, if something bad happened, I might have a tendency to try and hit a driver on the next hole when I shouldn't be and get a little aggressive and make things happen. And right now, I am able to, like I said, sustain the good play through the round and remain patient.

Q. So, your confidence is different?

A. Yeah. I think the biggest thing is that I can continue to play good all the way through the round and that gives me confidence. And when you're hitting more greens, you think you're going to make more birdies. In golf, everything kind of seems to feed on itself. If you're hitting the ball well and putting well, the rest seems to get better, too. So, you shoot better scores. It all comes down to consistency. And I think I am just more consistent. Part of it is mental and part of it's physical.

Q. So, your short game has changed?

A. One thing that I have noticed is I don't have the three putts. My putting is a lot more rounded. I am making a lot of five and six footers. I am making a lot more than I had in the past.

Q. What would you say about the treatment in terms of convenience, pain or discomfort?

A. Going through the treatment was really the easiest part. It was painless and fast, and it was definitely something that could only help you.

Q. Would you recommend it to golfers?

A. I would recommend it. I think that through my own experience, there's no doubt that I have become better, and my game is more rounded. And I think everybody can use that in their golf game. Even if you get a little bit out of it instead of a lot, it's something that could help your game.

B.S. male golf professional

Q. Since you have had (Performance Integration℠) treatment, has there been any affect in your golf game that you're aware of?

A. Well, I am much more relaxed. My concentration seems to be a little better. When I do hit a bad shot, I don't get upset anymore, which is very nice.

Q. How about your particular enjoyment of the game. Has there been any affect on that?

A. I don't feel like I have to practice as much as I used to and still be able to go out and hit good shots and be confident all the time on the course.

Q. What's the difference that allows you to do less practice?

A. I don't know. I wish I could give you a definite answer on that. I just — I think some of it had to do with the integration. I can jump up on the practice tee now and take five and six swings and be loose, whereas before, I used to have to hit fifty to sixty balls to get loose.

Q. So, could you recommend integration?

A. Sure I would recommend integration to anybody. Very simple, painless, real easy process to go through.

Q. And it makes a difference?

A. It seems to have, yes. Seems to have made a good difference. I seem to be a lot more relaxed.

R.H. female occasional golfer

A. I am married to a golf professional. I started playing golf about 10 years ago socially. I watch a lot of golf. I enjoy golf, and I feel like I have pretty good golf knowledge, but was a little bit frustrated that I could play with ladies 20 years older than I who could hit the ball better and I didn't quite understand what that was. I went and played golf one day, for the first time in a year and shot my normal score that I had been shooting five and six years ago, consistently. Then the next week I started some treatments, some Performance Integration℠ treatments, went out again to play golf with my children, and my husband came to watch me tee off and as I teed off on the first hole I hit probably the best drive I have ever hit in my life. I hadn't warmed up on the driving range at all, and my husband, the pro, was amazed. He said he had never seen that swing from me, and the only thing we could attribute that to was the Performance Integration℠. I hadn't practiced. I hadn't been playing, and he felt like I was finally putting together what he had been trying to tell me to do all along. I went and played golf with my children and improved my score by eight strokes from the previous week. I have since played golf again with a group of ladies that had seen me play before, and they were amazed at the difference just in two weeks of my shot making. I was straighter. I was more consistent. I wasn't missing as many shots. And I am not a good golfer. I am just a real average golfer, and I just feel it is through the Performance Integration℠ because it's not through practicing on the driving range. And the last few times I played, I have pulled out my seven iron and been able to hit a decent iron shot. I have always been afraid of my irons because I just choked with them.

Q. How about the way you feel about playing golf?

A. Well, after playing regularly for four years and not seeing any improvement and having to just be satisfied to have a good time, now I can't wait to get out there because now I feel that I have the ability to improve my game and become a decent golfer. Before integration, I basically was in a rut or at a certain level. I didn't expect to improve because I thought if I was going to improve, I would have improved through four years of regular play. I didn't even go hit balls on the driving range anymore because I didn't see the need. When I did hit practice balls, it didn't seem to improve my game at all. In fact, I couldn't hit them off the driving range any better than I could hit them on the golf course. So, I basically had abandoned practice. Since integration, and since I saw some improvement in my game, I have now been to the driving range. I am now seeing a reason to go out and practice. I am excited about it. I am excited about learning to use more of my clubs in the bag instead of just the two or three that I felt comfortable with.

P.W. female serious golfer

Q. Would you make any general statement about your golf game before and after Performance Integration^{SM}?

A. Before integration, I know prior to competition I would be very nervous. I think I lacked a lot of confidence. I knew I could play the game, but I wasn't sure how I would tee it up. I would start getting doubts in my mind; therefore, I would be very nervous. After integration, I just completed a tournament in Sacramento, I was not nervous at all. I was so confident on the tee. I knew what I wanted to do. Now I am very confident, and I am not nervous at all prior to competition. I am fine.

Q. What is it about your game that has changed?

A. Confidence. I am hitting the ball straighter. I just feel very confident. I don't have doubts like I used to. I would doubt that I was a player at times, and now I know I can do it. I am very confident. The biggest word is confidence. That's it.

Q. What would you say about your long game, specifically?

A. I have always been a strong wood player prior to integration. And after integration, it's continued. It hasn't changed at all. What has improved is my iron play. I am striking the irons better now than I used to. That was always my weak link. My husband, jokingly, said that I am a three handicap with a wood in my hand, but I am a thirty-six with an iron in my hand. And that is just so true. But, now, I am doing much better with my irons, and I am still not equal to the woods, but I have improved considerably. I have seen a huge improvement on iron play. And my current handicap is an eight. And I expect to be down to a six, five or six by the end of the season, and I think I will be there. I am more consistent with scoring. I think this has really helped. I feel a huge difference in this integration. And the biggest thing is confidence, not being nervous.

Q. Good. What would you say about your mental game? Is that a confidence thing?

A. Now, I am still not practicing like I should, but I feel better prepared. I know that I can make the stroke, and I just know it's going to happen. So, I am not even worried about it. Before, I used to worry and be a little stressed on trying to compete with the other better players in our area because they would practice and I wouldn't and then I would hit the tee really unprepared. But now, I am hitting the tee the same way, but I feel very prepared in my mind, which is the mental part of the game. I feel much more prepared than I did before, and I am still not practicing. If I could just practice, I think I would really be a threat to some people. But the integration has helped me big time on that. If I would use one word to describe the benefits of integration, it would be confidence. Confidence and handling stress for me.

Q. What did you think of the treatment?

A. Excellent. I would recommend it to anyone. I think it's just excellent.

Q. Painful?

A. No, no, not painful at all. I have always had problems with my muscles right here in my arms. If I don't play golf for three or four days, and when I swing, it would be like swinging a two by four, and it would hurt. And, now, I never have a pain. Ever since integration, it's gone. I don't play for four days, I can pick up the wood and I can swing away without any problem at all. And that's a huge difference, too.

J.W. male frequent and now serious golfer, P.G.A. administration

A. I just couldn't wait to see how good I could play with integration. Consequently, I think I was expecting a lot to happen to go from an 88 shooter down to a 78 shooter overnight, and that didn't happen. But as I started playing everyday, a strange thing happened, which I didn't know was happening and I couldn't really put my finger on it, but my peers —people I played with, asked me why all of a sudden I was making a proper turn at the ball. And I said, "Well, I don't know. I'm not doing anything different." And they said, "Well, you are. You are, finally, after 20 years, you are making the proper turn." And consequently, I was hitting the ball a lot further. Well, it just happened. I noticed some changes when other people actually said I was making a bigger turn, and I thought about it. And I was making the shoulder and the hip turn, which professionals have been trying to get me to do for 14 years, and I have not been able to do it. I don't know why, but I am the classic swayer. I sway away from it, and I sway into it. Now, I am turning, and I am hitting the ball just unbelievably well. Thank you.

Q. Say something, specifically, about the affects on your long game?

A. Well, again, the effects — I am hitting the ball —it has to be 30 yards further than normal. And the fun thing about this, the really fun thing about it is not only the results but the pleasure you receive from accomplishing that and hitting the ball the way you are supposed to. And for me, personally, it has been a struggle to get that ball in play, that very first shot in play. And now, I am hitting the fairways with more regularity. I mean, I am even counting how many fairways I hit just for the fun of it. And when you hit fairways, it's much easier to pull out that iron and be hitting off of a short grass into a green, and the confidence level is there. I mean, once you start striking the ball with consistency and accuracy that just overlaps into the short game and naturally you start hitting more greens. I don't think about that any more. I am so elated that my ball is in play. It's not in the rough. It's not OB. It's not in the water, out to the right. I am a classic slicer of the ball. I cast the club instead of swing the club. So, yes, the answer to your question, I am hitting more greens. I am having a lot more fun and the stress is gone and the enjoyment is immense.

Q. What was the treatment like?

A. He hits key spots on your body which he determines through a scientific method, and he stimulates those spots and you can immediately see the change in your strength, and that's what's apparent. The physical appearance is that you can witness the strength right then and there, and that's what is amazing. The wonderful thing, on a day-to-day basis, is the lack of stress and the total concept of feeling in charge of your body. I don't know how to really, really stress that I am in charge now. I feel good. I feel energetic. I am aware of things. I am on top of things, and that's a power feeling. You're not controlled by any needs to do something. You are in charge, and if something requires your reference, you're there 100 percent energetically, mentally and physically. You are charged. And boy, I just love this feeling. I can't wait to live from day to day. I love each day's different experience because I am in charge. I am living. It — it's not happening. I am living.

J.U. female golf professional

Q. Tell us about your golf experience following integration.

A. And after our sessions with the integration, I found that first of all, it was during the wintertime so I couldn't get out. I had the longest layoff that I have ever had from golf this winter, which was approximately four months. So, when I picked up the clubs again, I really didn't know what to expect. In the past, when it has even been one month, it felt foreign really having the club in my hand again. But this time, I was able to feel the swing sooner, and I am hitting the ball better than I ever have been now that I have had a chance to get out three and four times a week. So, I am real pleased with that.

Q. What would you say, specifically, about your long game? How has that been affected, if at all?

A. I found that I am making better contact with the driver, and the ball is going probably 10 to 15 yards longer. When I stand over the ball for the short game, I just have a real feeling of knowing what I want to do with the club. Whereas before, there have been times where I stand there and go "which option do I want"? Now, I feel like the option is almost right there in the front of my mind. So, that should definitely take off some strokes on the game.

Q. What can you say about confidence?

A. Well, you know, when you start playing well, it helps your confidence. And I felt — I can't tell you how great I felt after I played those nine holes a couple days ago. And I did feel real confident that I am ready to go out.

Q. What kind of statement would you make about what Performance Integration[SM] has done to your golf game?

A. I would say Performance Integration[SM] has given me inner confidence and inner sense of trust that I am able to go out there and play as well as I want to play any time I want to play under any kind of conditions. And I believe that people have skills in golf, but unless they have trust in those skills, they can't accomplish anything; and I feel now I have the trust in and those skills.

A. I think it really is something that will be beneficial to anyone that has aspirations for being successful out there playing. I really believe that this allows me to go out there, and if I am in a situation — and even if I am having a bad day, which this isn't to say that you're never going to have a bad day playing golf, you can still get a perspective that this was just a bad day, and that's to be there, to be expected; but the good days are so much better that you don't really worry about the bad ones any more. I really believe in it, or I wouldn't be sitting here right now. Something happened, and it's hard to understand, but I don't know if understanding is the way to approach it as much as to accept. And I accept a change has been made for the better.

Q. How would you recommend it?

A. I recommend that if they are looking — if they feel that they've heard all there is to be heard, how to set up and how to do the mechanical part of golf that if they really want to truly feel an understanding for the game, and the correct techniques, they might try this to get the correct feeling inside to allow them to really hear what is being said in the lessons. Sometimes the intenseness and the fear doesn't really allow them to hear what we're saying. I think I would recommend this to anyone that says to me I really want to get better at this game, and I think this might be a key component to allowing them to get better, and it's worth a try.

R.C. male insurance executive, serious golfer

Q. Tell me about what affect you noticed, if any, in your golf game?

A. My golf game has been great. I particularly noticed it on the short game. The short game has been a lot better. I noticed markedly putting had been changed. But more than the putting, the chipping, the general short game, the intenseness of the game, maybe the concentration has been better, but I know one thing, I have picked up a couple strokes on my handicap. I have to attribute it to the short game more than anything.

Q. Can you describe a difference in your level of confidence or the level of concentration?

A. I guess more of a mellowness that I have had, more of a feeling that things are just happening because I am a little bit more in control of my feelings, a little bit more in control in my game when it comes to golf, a little bit more in control of my life, a little bit more in control of my sales presentations, a little bit more confident. It's not so markedly different. We're not talking about fifty percent nor a hundred percent, but there is definitely a change, and I feel good about it, and I am glad I did it.

J.M. male advertising executive, serious golfer

Q. You have been through the P.I. program. Tell me, have you noticed any change in your life since you have been through the program?

A. Yeah, I have. It is amazing to me, and I noticed it right away, the mellowness. I am able to handle tense situations a lot better now than I have in the past, better able to deal with them in the business that I am in. They happen every day. I think its mellowed me out some.

Q. What about your golf game? Have you noticed any difference in your games since you went through P.I.?

A. Yeah. It screwed me up. It screwed me up, and I'll tell you how in a positive way. I — finally, I get more distance on the ball now. I hit the ball further, and so I have had to adjust. I have had to adjust what clubs I use from what distance. I have had to adjust my game around the green. Now that I know, now that I have played with it, and I feel comfortable with it, my handicap has gone down four. I was a 14, now I am a 10.

Q. Okay. On the critical part of golf, the short game, the approach shots, the chips, the putting, is there anything that you are consciously aware of that is different now?

A. Mentally I have always had a good short game. That is the thing that saved my golf. But now, I don't think — if I think I am on the fringe of the green, I literally think I can put it in the hole. Before, my goal was to get it close. It's not that way any more. I think I can put it in the hole.

Q. When you are standing over a putt, any difference in attitude, any difference in feeling?

A. I feel there isn't a putt that I can't put in. There isn't one too long anymore. I have a lot more confidence around the green than I am even used to. I have always had confidence around the green, but where it had helped me, literally, is on my mid-iron shots and off the tee because there is a big difference between hitting a four iron into the green, and a six iron into the green. And now, off the tee, I am hitting the ball far enough that I am not using long irons. I am using mid-range irons or shorter irons. And so, I have more control, and so I am getting the ball closer, and I think that's what has been helping my handicap. I am getting closer to the pin.

Q. Would you recommend it to other golfers?

A. Oh, absolutely. I wouldn't even hesitate to. In fact, I have. I have got two or three golfers who would like to go through it because they have seen what it has done to my game, and they can't believe it. I beat them now.

A.C. female stock broker, serious golfer

Q. Let's talk about your golf game. You have been through the program. What has happened to you?

A. The most specific thing I notice is when I stand up to hit the ball, I used to go through a mental chain of thoughts. It was a process of take the club back, take it back low. It was a complete chain. Now, I seem to stand up and hit it. It has all come together. It's not a chain of thoughts. It's just one motion, and it has just come together for me, that way.

Q. Tell me, is there any difference that you have noticed in that experience looking down that fairway?

A. Well, maybe, again, the concentration. The ability to look down the fairway and to stay with it, to see — maybe to visualize and concentrate on the game a little bit more. By the way, my drives are going a whole lot further because my swing is looser because I am not going through those segments.

Q. Having been through the Performance Integration℠ program now, about your short game? Is there any difference?

A. That has improved as well. Chipping, I think, is tremendous — good chipping, as a result of concentration again, and thinking about where you want the ball to land rather than just trying to hit the green, and I seem now to be able to concentrate more on placing the ball rather than just getting it there. Now, I seem to be able to concentrate more and think it through.

Q. Putting?

A. Putting. I don't know if that will ever get better. I really haven't noticed much difference with the putting. Putting is a problem for me. I may have a mental block on that.

Q. Other people you have played golf with, has anybody commented on it?

A. Everyone — everyone has commented. Well, most of my girlfriends just can't believe how well I am playing. My husband and I played in Arizona, and we played match play, the two of us on a brand new course, and I beat him for the first time in our entire life. I did. I beat him.

J.M. male advertising executive, serious golfer, one year after Performance Integration^{SM}

A. I have a better feel for my driver. I am hitting the ball longer, and I am more consistently in the fairway. I'm not flirting with the fringes. I am talking about — I'm really in position where I want to be to hit the green.

Q. Are you on the green in regulation more frequently?

A. Yes. That's the key to my game. The change between now and before I started this program, before I would probably be on 10 greens out of 18, and I had to rely on my chipping to save par. I can literally say in 18 holes, now, that I am on the green 15 to 17 greens in 18 holes.

Q. Has your total putts per round changed?

A. Yes, but not because I am sinking putts. What I am doing is I am lagging a lot better. I am getting closer to the hole on my first putt. I'm not leaving myself hard second putts. Consequently my score has gone down because I have been able to sink the short putt.

Q. Has the accuracy of your shot changed long and short game?

A. The accuracy of my long shots has changed tremendously. I literally feel confident over the ball where I can put it on the green where I want it. My short game has always been great, and I haven't seen a change in my short game.

Q. Has your consistency changed in hitting the ball straighter?

A. No. I hit a slice, and I play from the slice, I am hitting further; but I'm not necessarily hitting straighter.

Q. Specifically, how has your long game been affected?

A. I drive the ball 15 to 20 yards further now than I used to.

Q. How has your short game been affected?

A. Not a lot other than I may be a little more consistent with it, but I always feel real good with my short game.

Q. How has your management of the game changed?

A. That's where I am starting to think better. I am thinking my way through a golf course now rather than just hitting the golf ball. And that's making a lot of difference in the way I play golf, which really has had a big affect on even how I approach certain holes.

Q. Has your joy of the game changed?

A. Absolutely. The better you play, the better, you know — I'm having the time of my life. I'm shooting better golf than I have ever played.

Q. What do you feel has been the difference in your golf game since Performance Integration℠?

A. The biggest difference has been I literally have been able to put my whole game together. I have got now what I consider a literally smooth integrated swing no matter where I am on the golf course. I'm even hitting long irons now where I never could before. I couldn't hit two and three irons, and now they're comfortable. They feel good. That part of my game has really changed.

Q. How often have you been playing since your integration?

A. Once or twice a week.

Q. Is that more or less than usual?

A. That's a little more.

Q. Was the Performance Integration℠ responsible for any of the changes you have noted?

A. About 80 per cent of them.

Q. Do you have an established handicap?

A. Yes, it's eight.

Q. Has your handicap changed since your Performance Integration℠?

A. Yes, I was a 14.

Q. Have there been any changes in you body that occurred following Performance Integration℠?

A. Yes, I've had a chronic backache for about 24 years. This is literally the first time that I have been going from morning until night without hurting.

Q. How has — how have those changes affected you, your life, your golf game?

A. My life, I'm just more in control, and I think that's the same thing about my golf game. I mean both of them are more in control.

Q. Has your ability to handle stress changed since your Performance Integration℠?

A. Yes. I am — it's not that I am much more mellow, I am just as intense. I just deal with it differently, and I don't know how to explain that. I just — I handle situations differently now than I used to.

Q. Was the Performance Integration℠ Treatment painful, uncomfortable or inconvenient?

A. Not at all.

J.E. male insurance broker, serious golfer

Q. Explain to us what your experience has been that you can relate directly to the integration treatment that you have received. How has it affected your life, play, whatever?

A. Well, specifically, in my golf game, I noticed that for the past six to eight weeks, I strike the ball so much better, so much cleaner than I had before. Before, I had what I would like to call a fade, but it was probably a slice, and it was due to the fact that I was not in balance, and I wasn't striking the ball cleanly. After this integration technique, I found that probably after the first couple of weeks, I started to strike the ball very well, very cleanly, and I am hitting the ball longer off the tee. I used to be 20 yards behind some of my compatriots. Now, I am out with them and beyond them.

Q. How soon after you received the treatment did you perceive that particular golf change?

A. Probably two weeks to a month because I think shortly after I started taking the treatments, I was trying too hard. I was trying to use whatever I had to make it work instead of letting it take hold and letting it work. I think my first game, I played very well, and then the next couple of games after that I played very poorly because I thought I new it all, and I could make it work instead of letting it work for me.

Q. You played a lot of golf several years ago?

A. Yes.

Q. Has this brought you back to the good golf experience you had or changed it?

A. It's brought me back to where I am striking the ball as well. I am not scoring as well as I had two or three years ago simply because I am not practicing, but I go out and play every — I mean once every ten days, and I notice that I am hitting the ball much more cleanly and much more specifically. I am hitting it where I want to. It's when I am get around the greens that I — where the practice takes hold that I need more practice.

Q. Then have you not seen much change in the short game?

A. No, that's specifically because I have not practiced.

Q. But your long game has changed?

A. Oh, it's amazing. I am hitting par five's and par two's like I used to.

Q. Now, has any other part of your life been affected by this, do you think?

A. Yes. My energy level has increased somewhat. I can't tell you the degree or the percentage. I notice that I am more productive and seem to be a little bit more organized as a result of this. It may be partially mental and — but I am sure it's partially integration.

Q. Has anyone else noticed any changes in your golf lessons?

A. Yes, the people I play with.

Q. That's good. Now, going back to the treatment, itself. In the actual experience of the treatment, let's talk about whether it was comfortable, painful.

A. Oh, it was very comfortable. There was no pain involved at all. It was just a matter of moving, integrating and making it work. I felt no pain whatsoever. In fact, it was kind of enjoyable.

Q. Is there anything else you want to say, or how do you feel about recommending the treatment for golfers?

A. Oh, I fully recommend it to those who are very frustrated with their games, who feel they need to improve and maybe some of these self teachers should probably take a look at this kind of thing in order to improve their games.

B.A. male amateur

Q. Would you tell us what kinds of experiences you had relating to changes specifically in your athletic endeavors?

A. I noticed first after the treatment that it seemed that my concentration increased. I was able to pinpoint more on what I was working on better which carried over to my golf game. Golf is mostly mental anyway, I think. So, I was able to concentrate on the ball and forget about everything else. Therefore, I am playing better now, it seems.

Q. Specifically, how has your golf game changed, the long game and short game?

A. Mostly off the tee. I am a lot, lot longer off the tee. My mental errors are basically fewer which is my biggest problem before I get up to the ball, and I just kind of like forget what I was doing. Now, I am able to concentrate. My whole golf game has picked up.

Q. Talk about the affect it has had specifically in your short game?

A. My irons and chipping, I am getting much closer to the pin. I am still a terrible putter, but my chipping is much better. I am closer to the pin. On my second shots, I am hitting the green more often.

Q. Have you been able to play a lot of golf lately?

A. No, not as much as I would like, which to play good golf, you need to play often. I am very busy, so I haven't had a lot of time to play, but that's kind of why it has surprised me that I am playing as well as I am because I haven't had a lot of time to practice or play.

Q. In the past, have you experienced any kind of a schooling or teaching or practice that gave you this kind of an experience?

A. Not really. If I ever took a lesson or something, it seemed like during the lesson I could do it, but I get to where I was going, and the same thing — I couldn't concentrate as well, and I would fuzz right through the whole situation.

Q. Now, when you did the integration treatment, how soon after the treatment do you think it changed?

A. Actually, my golf game didn't really pick up until recently that I noticed so much. I notice my stamina increased right off. I ride bicycles also, and I noticed that right off that I could ride harder and faster than I ever could before. And just recently, my golf game has been picking up.

A. I just think it has probably made me a little more low key, laid back and not worry about it as much, which relaxes me in golf. You have to be relaxed in golf. I think that has helped me a lot.

Q. Talking about the treatment. What did you think about the treatment, and how did you feel going through the treatment physically?

A. I was a little skeptical at first, but I am just that kind of person. I went in with an open mind. It was very quick and painless, you know, very quick and painless. I was hoping for the best. It seemed to work out okay.

Q. Now, if you were to isolate this treatment as a specific entity, how would you feel about recommending it to golfers or athletes?

A. I would recommend it. I would recommend it for concentration. That's all I know for sure. It helped my concentration immensely. It helped me sharpen up, and if anybody has some problems, of course in golf you need to be very mentally alert, I would say definitely go for it. It doesn't hurt you at all. If anything, it will benefit you. I recommend it.

G.R. male golf professional

A. All my statistical aspects of my game have improved, and I feel very comfortable with the ball now. It's very easy for me to get comfortable with the ball which has been a problem.

A. Now that my balance has improved, my focus has improved, I finally gained 30 yards off the tee with increase of accuracy, consistently at 260, 270 as opposed to a 260 then a 240. So, it's a consistent distance now.

A. After the Performance Integration℠, without changing any of my work habits, as far as working on my game is concerned, my game jumped up a level.

K.M. serious golfer, father of teen serious golfers

A. My daughter, Carrie, has been through the program. The main improvement that we have seen is in her basic coordination. She plays golf as a sport. She plays competitively. We had noticed kind of a lack of coordination and kind of a lack of strength that we were worried about.

She went through the program and almost immediately we could see changes in Carrie's coordination her stability and her power in playing.

She definitely became more powerful. Almost immediately, she became more powerful. I would say probably— she added 10 to 15 percent to her distance.

K.G. male, mechanical engineer, serious golfer

Q. Tell me what it was that motivated you to pursue the program with the Performance Integration℠?

A. Well, it had to do with golf, actually, and I had goals of trying to get a handicap in the single digits and couldn't seem to get it there regardless of what I did. I went through the program, and I am down in that range now. I haven't had any lessons, or anything since then, and I haven't seemed to be doing anything differently. I cut five or six strokes off my handicap in the process of doing it. So, I was really the motivated.

Q. That's great. What do you think went on with you that helped make this change? How did the change occur?

A. I think it had a lot to do with the concentration.

It seems that things come more easily than they were before with less concentration on thoughts involved with doing the sport.

Q. What was the change in your body?

A. Again, I think it was coordination. When you hit a bad golf shot you can feel it in your swing once you have done it. I was able to groove my swing more consistently than I was before. The bad shots still come, but not as frequently, and it seems that the swing is much more consistent than before. I am more coordinated. Less concentration required to get the swing is the feeling I have.

Q. State something about what your original handicap was and what it is now?

A. It was 14 or 15 before, and it's somewhere probably between 9 and 10 right now. I haven't taken any lessons since that point. I can't attribute it to anything else. I have had problems previously with tee shots a lot, losing the tee shot. You lose a tee shot, and you are in a lot of trouble on a lot of courses period. I have been able to keep them on the fairway a lot more consistently and that seemed to help my game.

Q. What was your perception of the treatment as you look through it? How did you feel about it, think about it?

A. Well, I'll tell you, I'll have to say that when we first began treatment, I was skeptical about it. As things went along and since then, I have done a little bit of reading on it, I think there is much more to it scientifically than I originally thought.

Q. So, you say you perceived some changes in the long and the short game?

A. The swing, whether it's the tee shots, whether it's the long game or the short game, I can keep the swing the same tempo and the same, you know, rhythm to the swing that I wasn't able to do before. You know when you can do things consistently, the same, then the golf ball is going to go the right way. Since then, I have been able to do that. It's more coordinated effort without the concentration, intense concentration, I thought, that was required to make myself do it. It's easier and smoother, more coordinated, I feel. The frustration level wasn't there.

Q. Now, how do you feel about recommending the treatment?

A. I definitely recommend it, especially along the lines of golf. I still think that lessons are not something you want to give up for the treatment, but I think that it definitely coordinated me and anything that I do to bring my game up from here on in will just benefit what's happened from the coordination I received from the treatment.

TOP GOLFERS

Research and development of the ultimate protocol called Performance Integration℠ extends back to the first efforts of man to spear a fish, hurl an axe or any other art requiring brain/body coordination. Man's efforts to be better, to enhance his survival and improve his outcomes testify of the marvelous mechanisms of self-actualization.

People who truly want to be better, do better, have better, and are willing to reach to accomplish that are truly a thrill to work with. The Top Golfers quoted throughout this text are like that. They are doers and achievers. They wanted to be, do, and have better, and when introduced to Performance Integration℠ they said "lets go for it". Their candid expression of their outcome and experience following Integration treatment are from the heart as well as the rest of their brain/body. Their full names are not cited because it was deemed unnecessary, but their experiences are available for appropriate scrutiny. The following is a list of all those cited along with some identifiers.

A.C. 49, female, Stock broker, serious golfer

A.D. 28, female, Aerobics instructor, sales

A.W. 35, male, Golf professional, golf management

B.A. 32, male, Golf course manager, frequent golfer

B.G. 65, male, Retired executive, serious golfer

B.H. 42, male, Golf professional, instructor

B.M. 59, male, Real Estate broker, golfer

B.S. 43, male, Golf professional, instructor

C.L. 38, male, Golf professional, instructor

C.M. 12, female, Serious golfer

D.H. 40, female, Travel management, occasional golfer

G.R. 37, male, Golf professional, instructor

J.E. 53, male, Insurance agent, serious golfer

J.G. 48, male, Professional aviator

J.M. 45, male, Advertising executive, serious golfer

J.U. 45, female, Golf professional, instructor

J.W. 52, male, Golf management, serious golfer

K.G. 30, male, Mechanical engineer, serious golfer

K.W. 35, female, Golf professional, instructor

L.E. 41, female, Serious golfer

M.M. 32, male, Golf professional, golf management

N.D. 54, male, Construction executive

N.L. 50, male, Radio personality, serious golfer

P.L. 42, male, Golf professional, golf management

P.W. 46, female, Golf management, serious golfer

R.C. 49, male, Insurance executive, serious golfer

R.C. 60, male, Ski coach, skier

R.H. 39, female, Frequent golfer

R.T. 46, male, Advertising, occasional golfer

S.W. 45, female, Bank executive, frequent golfer

T.M. 16, male, Serious golfer

ABOUT THE AUTHOR

Dr. Clyde Porter has been on the cutting edge of natural health care since 1977. Beginning as a Wholistic Doctor of Chiropractic, he has used a variety of techniques and therapies to help people not only get well, but achieve optimum health. In 1985, Dr. Porter began work in the field of neurologic integration. Researching body/brain communication challenges from dyslexia to jet pilot performance, his studies have taken him across the United States. His Performance Integration℠ work has enriched the lives of individuals ranging from infants to senior citizens, including military aviators, professional athletes, business leaders, and others seeking the best their body and mind have to give.

Dr. Porter has lectured widely on peak performance and optimum health and well-being. An innovator in the field of human neurologic integration, he has helped thousands of people achieve performance levels and a quality of life they never thought possible.

ORDER FORM

For additional copies of TOP GOLF call Toll Free 1-800-803-9235
Have your AMEX, Visa, Mastercard ready

Fax Orders: (702) 331-0192

Postal Orders: Life Enhancement Services
                     P.O. Box 3236
                     Sparks, Nevada   89432

Price: $14.95

Sales Tax: Add 7% for books shipped to Nevada

Shipping: $3.00 for the first book and $0.75 for each additional
book to the same location
Overnight $4.00 per book

Payment:
Credit card ____ Visa, ____ Mastercard, ____ AMEX Card

Number:_____

Expiration Date _____

Name on card: _____

Send me dates and locations for Performance Integration℠ clinics.

Address:_____

_____

_____